DISASTER PASTOR

The Power of a Small Light

Rev. Dr. Toby Nelson

Third Edition

Dedication

To my wife, Judy

Thou art all fair my love;

there is no flaw in thee.

Song of Solomon 4:7

Table of Stories

Report 1   The Gift

The work and calling of a Disaster Pastor is a Terrible-Honor.

This book will take you where you likely have never been before. Many of the stories are dark, some are funny and all are meant to be inspirational and instructional.

My hope is to give you a gift, it is the skill of listening for the Human Cry. Solomon had this skill; he is considered the wisest man in the Old Testament. After his father, David, died, Solomon ascended to the Throne to become King of Israel. God visited him. In their conversation God says, "Ask for whatever you want me to give you." There are a number of things that come to my mind if God gave me that offer. This famous story becomes all the more remarkable by Solomon's answer.

"Give me a heart that listens...."[1]

The disaster stories that follow are intended to increase your skill of specifically listening to the Human Cry.

And, I hope you will vicariously test yourself by asking the question that lies beneath just below the surface:

"What would I have done?" The final words of this book end that this question.

---

[1] 1 Kings 3.5,9

Report 2   Listening To The Unthinkable

One of the teams on which I was serving deployed to a destination where thousands had fled their seaside homes. Among the many, a young adult sat cross-legged on a cot, barely two inches above the filth and waste that spread across the floor.

This woman had no shoes; her clothing was caked with mud; and her thick black hair, peppered with small bits of debris, hung stiffly across her shoulders. She was squeezed among those who found this shelter after the tsunami destroyed their homes and way of life. One of the medics finished treating a deep cut on her back and signaled with his hand that she and I needed to meet.

"Would you visit that young woman?" asked the medic. He pointed to a woman in a blue shirt with an infant in her lap. He walked away to treat others requiring medical attention. I began stepping around a dozen cots with a hundred family members clustered around them, in order to reach the woman.

"Hello, Miss," I said, "I am a Chaplain." I knelt down in the slick, putrid sludge spread across the concrete floor. Not knowing her story, I smiled and gently said, "Please, tell me your name." For a traumatized person, it is a fact question that is easy to answer.

"Mariana," she replied vacantly.

"Is this your son?" She nodded. The boy, draped over her lap like a rag doll, was asleep. Absent-mindedly, she traced random patterns on his back with intermittent caresses to his head, down his neck, then back to the random movements across his back. "Tell me what happened."

"The tsunami," she simply said. This tsunami had pushed ashore with a 23 foot wave of ocean water and had rapidly consumed the dry land and houses in less than two minutes.

"Last night," she began slowly. Obviously she was exhausted but wanted to tell her story. "We barely escaped." She paused to wipe away tears. "I only had time to grab my twin boys, one under each arm." She shaped both arms, as if she still carried the two 25-pound children.

Twin boys? "Where is the other boy?" I wondered, but waited to ask. Denying the obvious, I silently prayed, "Oh, Lord, I hope she did not have to...." She read my puzzled face.

"It was dark and so windy," she explained softly. "The water was up to my chest. The current pulled so hard, I couldn't move forward. There was no one to help me."

She slumped forward over her son and with the palms of her hands, wiped away more tears. I imagined, a slightly built young mother, bobbing in the cold dark water, struggling to keep her boys' heads above the rising deluge.

Exhaustion overwhelmed her heroic efforts. Spent, she was steadily losing her grip on the twins. The powerful roiling waters removed the possibility of her swimming with the two heavy boys clutched under her arms. She was in a no-win situation and had precious little time to consider the consequences – only another second to decide.

"It felt like hours," she said, gasping for air as she choked out her story. "My boys were wet and slippery. My arms could no longer keep their heads from going under water. I just couldn't make it... with both."

Pushed beyond depletion and desperation, she was forced to think the unthinkable. Violating her maternal instincts, she loosened her grip and released one of her sons into the dark swirling water.

Consumed with pain and shame, Mariana huddled over her surviving boy, sobbing convulsively. This grieving mother's dreadful choice was already in the past. Her big brown eyes, endlessly flooding with tears, pleaded for me to make sense of her loss … and her actions.

What should I say? The only words Mariana really wanted to hear were, "I can bring back your other son." That was not going to happen.

I mentally scanned through a flipchart of platitudes that trauma victims often use to comfort themselves. Well-meaning sympathizers use these same platitudes in the attempt to comfort survivors and victims. Several statements that I have actually heard people say come to mind. Each time I hear these statements, I cringe.

Statements like:

"God won't give us more than we can handle."

"That which does not kill us makes us stronger."

"You should have trusted God to give you strength.

After all, the Bible promises, 'I can do all things through Christ who strengthens me.'"

"You shouldn't feel that way."

"You were his mother. How could you let go of your own child?"

"If you confess your sin of letting your boy go, God will be faithful and forgive you."

"I know exactly what you are going through. Let me tell you my story."

One inane thought I had with Mariana was, "Maybe God rescued your boy and he is safe somewhere." I held my tongue, realizing that false hope can be worse than saying nothing.

Giving these kind of platitudes that have inserted themselves into our modern culture like spiritual viruses actually often hurt and anger those we are longing to comfort. The truth is that terrible and dark events happen and platitudes offer no light for understanding.

Sometimes, even traumatized people may use these platitudes as coping mechanisms to survive, so I do not chide anyone for their own chosen management style. However, we need to remember that they too need comfort from us, not correction.

The best alternative I have found is for us to remain attentively silent, to say nothing and just listen. After a person has told me their story I choose to remain quiet and wait for them to say more, to reveal questions and pain. This is the best strategy especially in the beginning our conversations.

An immediate benefit is that it prevents us from saying anything inappropriate or hurtful. Sometimes the most powerful messages we give are the ones we give without words. In the Old Testament, Solomon wrote, "Death and life are in the power of the tongue..."[2]

---

[2] Proverbs 18.21 NIV

Our silence also gives the person time to hear what they just said and begin to grasp the fragments of their experience and string them into coherent thoughts. Silence is the best initial response 90% of the time. A nod of the head is enough to communicate you heard what was said.

Resist the temptation to ask questions early in your conversations with survivors. Remain silent and listen as people verbalize their stories. It is best for people to tell what happened without requiring them to relive the trauma. Hopefully, they will have access to post-trauma therapy later.

One evening I was paired up the Sergeant Jason Perry when we were dispatched to an address where neighbors in an apartment building were shouting and threatening each other. We arrived to find two men arguing over a drug deal.

One felt cheated by the other. Another officer arrived as backup and the two men were separated and questioned. I stood behind Perry and watched him interact with his subject. I was amazed at how much information he gathered from the man.

"How did you get him to give up so much information?" I asked.

"Once he started talking I didn't interrupt him," answered Perry. I asked him to tell me more. "Inexperienced officers will ask a question every seven seconds."

"What's wrong with that?" I asked.

"I learn more by letting the person tell his story and just listening carefully," he explained. "When the man is finished, then I will ask questions to fill in the gaps or reveal inconsistencies."

Mariana had already made her decision. Her lost boy could not be brought back. What was done was done.

What did Mariana need to hear from me? When words become necessary, our voice must give grace to empower people to be free to move on. The next words out of my mouth would bring more death or life.

What she needed was to be relieved of her consuming guilt. She needed to be assured that she had made the right decision. She made the only decision she could make in the midst of the deep, roiling waters.

"Mariana, please look at me." Her head turned to face me and her soulful eyes were full of every sorrow and sadness. Her face expressed what her words could not.

"Mariana, you did the right thing," I declared.

She paused and sighed, then said, "Thank you. I needed to hear that." Mariana was released of a dark burden and could now focus on caring for her surviving son.

I offered to pray a blessing on her and she nodded her head. "Lord, thank you for saving Mariana and her son. We trust you to hold her other son in your loving arms. Amen." Her lips silently mouthed, "Amen."

"Thank you," she said quietly, with her words and her eyes. I stood up and moved on to yet another urgent voice. As a disaster pastor, I engage in these kinds of conversations, non-stop, fifteen to twenty-five a day... for days or weeks.

Report 3   The Voice In the Chapel

Fellow team members and I were gathered this night in preparation for deployment. The mood was alert but relaxed and our soft voices seemed to blend in with the indigenous bullfrogs and crickets, resulting in an odd sort of baritone choir.

After settling on a soft spot in the dirt to sleep, my eyes scanned the infinity of the night sky above. With the sky illuminated by starlight and the smells that accompany an outdoor evening, the majesty of the heavens above invited my soul to review events that brought me to this place. I fell under a reflective spell.

I was reminded in the Old Testament of David who wrote Psalms, poems describing a Voice that occasionally speaks on a silent night sky like the one above me:

> The heavens declare the glory of God;
> the sky displays his handiwork.
> Day after day it speaks out;
> night after night it reveals his greatness.
> There is no actual speech or word
> nor is its voice literally heard.
> Yet its voice echoes throughout the earth;
> its words carry to the distant horizon.[3]

---

[3] Psalm 19.1-4 NIV

The open vastness of the starry night seemed to loosen memories that had been suppressed by distractions for a long time. An event stood out more clearly in my mind than the bright stars in the night sky.

It was when I heard the Voice for the first time. That experience became a permanent bookmark in my brain ... a defining moment in my life. After three years of attending Trinity Evangelical Divinity School, a graduate seminary north of Chicago, I entered the seminary Chapel.

Alone in this sacred space, I quickly scanned the room. I wanted to make sure I was alone before I knelt at the altar, seeking the Lord and desperate for serious guidance. I had arrived at this posture on my knees because graduation for my Master's degree was less than a month a way.

Actually, I was panicked. My friends were landing nice positions and were about to enter secure futures in the ministry. Not me. On my knees in the Chapel, I was anxious. I was distraught. I looked again to make certain no one was in the Chapel before I bowed my head and closed my eyes to pray, to talk honestly and bluntly to God.

"Coming to seminary was your idea," I complained out loud to God. "I believed you led me here." My frustration boiled over and gave power to the seriousness of my grievance. "I trusted you and you are leaving me stranded." I was fed up with the silent treatment, the one-sided communication with God.

"If I were God for a day, I would make some changes," I thought. "Like, when people asked me questions... I would get back to them with an answer." Three years of seminary should have taught me to be polite with God. Apparently, I missed that lesson.

If God wanted me to pray and have a real relationship, then it was God's turn to talk. I always wondered if the silence of God was a way of hiding and not dealing with the likes of me. I was way past being nice to God. I was mad. After my rant burned off the pent up emotions, my insides fell quiet. Then, the Voice spoke.

"Toby, you do not have a great light."

Oh, no! Was I going to fail at ministry? This Voice was clearly recognizable, yet distinct from anything I had heard before. The Voice made my insides feel warm and at the same time it did not feel safe. It's tone was calm and direct.

It reminded me of a couple of famous actors whose vocal timbre sounded like what I would picture the voice of God, something like Charlton Heston, Sean Connery and probably more like James Earl Jones.

My senses were shocked by two realities: first, that God had an audible Voice. I know what I heard. The Bible is full of people who heard from God, but it never occurred to me that I might.

Inside my head there was something like an electronic message board crawling across the frontal lobe that read, "You are having a schizophrenic episode." From my studies in my college major, Psychology, I recalled one of the classic symptoms was hearing voices outside one's head.

Before I graduated, I was an intern at a mental facility. My ward had a dozen patients who carried on real conversations with George Washington, the Virgin Mary and Jesus. Was this my first episode of a dreadful mental illness? At 25 years old I was about the right age for onset of schizophrenia.

Whatever the source, this was a first for me. This is where my gift of denial helped. I decided I was not crazy.

The second reality struck me. The message was blunt. "God," I thought, "you should be nicer to me." I entered the Chapel devastated that no church wanted me. Now the Voice seemed to be piling on the negativity and rejecting me too. The Voice spoke again.

"I am sending you to dark places where your little light will shine brighter."

My light was defective, I thought. Perhaps that would explain why the churches never got back to me, that they too saw I had a little light in comparison to others.

Actually, I have always believed I was ill-suited for the ministry and know that my abilities are not typical for a Presbyterian pastor.

Maybe I had a little light because of my Attention Deficit Hyperactivity Disorder (ADHD), my occasional direct comments to sweet church ladies or my edgy sense of humor. Whatever the reason, the idea of serving in dark places had "missionary" written all over it. Fortunately, God's plan did not lead me toward darkest Africa - yet.

I waited on my knees for a while longer in case there were any more messages. I remained quiet and in the bowed position. Then, my knees began to really hurt.

The Voice was gone. The Silent One seemed to have retreated and resumed the familiar role of not speaking audibly. I left the Chapel.

In the next hour, I replayed the conversation over and over in my mind. I needed to remember the message correctly and not add to it or misunderstand it. I remember asking myself, "Did the Voice say I had a little light or a dim light?"

The term, little light, reminded me of the childhood song I learned in Sunday School, "This little light of mine, I'm going to let it shine…." I realized it was a special light and not a dim light.

I have heard that on a dark night and under the right atmospheric conditions, light from a candle can be seen from 10 miles away. In 1941 scientists from Columbia University documented that the human eye can see a lit candle 30 miles away.

Another more recent source shows that the human eye can see a 100 watt incandescent bulb over 60 miles.[4] Being told I have a little light was not the insult I initially thought; a little light can still go a long way.

Despite my conjectures, I knew that the Voice was not dismissing nor cursing me. Instead, it was giving me focus and identity. I did not know how this message would play out.

However, that Chapel meeting marked the beginning of countless, ongoing life-lessons that would teach me about darkness and the awesome power of a little light.

If I were to help change the world I needed learn how to use my little light. I began looking for dark places to serve.

About two weeks after hearing the Voice in the Chapel, a small Presbyterian church in the San Francisco Bay Area asked me to become their Youth Director. Although that sounded dark enough it turned out to an incredible ministry.

I do not hear the Voice often; actually only three more times in my life. The Voice would not always speak directly to me, but would use other mentors to transform my listening

---

[4] https://answers.yahoo.com/question/index?qid=20070915112857AAj3LzU

skills. I would learn to hear the Voice speak through tested and honorable people who were patient and kind in their training.

However, sometimes the Voice used two very harsh ones: Trial and Error. These two mentors proved painfully effective and were merciless when I did not listen to them.

Trial and Error took their turns at transforming me. Trial would drag me from one disaster to another; and Error felt like a bully pulling me from one room to another by my eyelids. Trial felt like a field goal kicker who took me into a small room and practiced drop kicking me. Each time I bounced off a wall I would loose my grip on a false truth that brought me no joy.

I tried speaking sweetly and asked *why* questions to these metaphorical masters, but they treated my complaints as signs of continued resistance. Error took his turn at manhandling me by holding me upside down until the last bit of nonsense was shaken out of me. Trial and Error had a specific goal: to train me to listen carefully for the voice of... the Human Cry.

Report 4   *Listening for the Human Cry*

"The Human Cry" is a phrase I coined to explain what is underneath the words people use to tell their stories. A Human Cry is the place of the deepest losses in our souls, losses that are so shameful that we will deny their existence before attempting to face and overcome them.

Everyone experiences a Human Cry, everyone: billionaires and beggars, ministers and warlords, heterosexuals and LBTGQ, First World and Third World citizens, saints and sinners ... everyone, regardless of their external appearances and despite all desperate pretenses to cover whatever cry lies deep inside.

How can you hear someone's Human Cry? We start with what Jesus advised, "Therefore, be careful how you listen."[5] This goes beyond active listening or deep listening, which often involves repeating what the person has just said. However, careful listening gives us clues to finding the Human Cry.

We do not interrupt the people by repeating what they just said. We allow them space to verbalize using their own words without imposing our own words and concepts.

---

[5] Luke 8:18 ASV

What does the Human Cry sound like? Sometimes when the person begins to express their Human Cry you may hear a sigh, that long, deep breath that is an audible signal of a yearning, a grief, a place of helplessness or hopelessness. They may repeat a word or phrase, endowing it with more feeling and deeper meaning.

A person's Human Cry is the driver in the self that demands satisfaction. The deep unmet needs of a person will become an emotional idol that must be served and demands sacrifice. Evidence of the Human Cry is usually seen with the manifestation of one or more of the seven deadly sins: anger, greed, sloth, pride, lust, envy and gluttony.

Stories may be the best way to understand the Human Cry. Listen not only for what people say aloud, but also for what is left unspoken, what is underneath the words of their stories.

Mariana wanted me to hear her Human Cry but was hesitant to verbalize it. It was that deep anguish in her soul that was crying to be heard, understood and healed. She desperately needed to know she was okay with God as she heard the life giving words, "You did the right thing."

I have experienced several Human Cries of my own. For example, at an extremely low point in my life, I was between jobs. For a few years I found myself unemployed. I had no prospect of any income, our savings account was empty, our credit cards were maxed out, the creditors began phoning and appearing at our front door. We were desperate for food, especially for our then fifteen-year old son. We would soon be homeless.

One day I found myself parked near the rear of a crowded Safeway grocery store. On the other side of my windshield was a worker standing at the end of the loading-dock throwing food into the dumpster. He tossed food that had passed its expired date or was blemished, the remains of the day. I was filled with envy that he had a fulltime paying job.

Well past closing time, I returned. Under the cover of darkness, I crept across the dock and peered into the dumpster. Before me were piles of usable, edible food. It became unsalable to customers who were willing to pay for more perfect appearing food. True, it was bruised and blemished, but what was piled before me was an abundance of vegetables and fruits at the peak of sweetness and taste. Among the boxes of food was an assortment of artisan breads for us to freeze and enjoy later.

That night I became a dumpster diver.

For the first time in my privileged life, I experienced a deep Human Cry, borne from something more painful than the physical hunger in my stomach. My specific Human Cry was my inability to provide basic needs for my family and my powerlessness to be free from my overwhelming shame and self-condemnation.

I wanted a job. Even though I had earned a Bachelors and a Masters degree, I saw myself only as a failed husband and father who could not provide food and possibly soon, shelter. My wife and son never complained or made me feel like a loser.

My self-condemnation was very capable of pointing out my shortcomings and failures. Life looks different viewed from the bottom of a dumpster.

It is hard to have pride when kneeling in garbage.

Dumpster diving was not just humbling; it was deeply humiliating. To me, I felt one step below begging and one step above stealing.

On a deeper level, circumstances of my own making served to shatter my inflated pride. Moreover, something wholesome happened when I realized my independent self-willed spirit had not served me well. David writes in the Psalms, "A broken and contrite spirit will not be despised by God."[6]

My time at the bottom of the dumpster took away my pretense, my charade of self-sufficiency. Standing in garbage made it easier to admit I had failed. As I bowed down to grab food, a wave of humiliation exorcized my hubris.

The box of food in front of me served as an altar where I surrendered my polished pretenses.

Finally, I was broken.

A short time later I took a phone call from a friend inviting me to work with him. It was a nice job that provided well for my family. Once again I was rescued and delivered us from destitution. However, I never forgot what it was like to have a devastating Human Cry. I hope I never forget how to listen for the Human Cry in those around me.

------

[6] Psalm 51.17

Report 5   Not Listening Can Kill

I almost killed a dear friend at a fire disaster. I love a fire ...
well, not the destructive side of a fire, but the energy, the
adrenaline rush and everything associated with wearing the
bunker suits of a real firefighter. Racing to a fire, unknown
details produce a certain amount of anxiety, hyper-awareness,
and the urgent need for any information that will let us know
what to expect at the site.

Are there people we might need to rescue? What
hazardous threats await us at the fire? As a volunteer fire
fighter in a small town in Mendocino County in northern
California, I came to realize that there is so much that remains
unknown until we have our boots down at the scene.

When the klaxon fire alarm would sound, it was like the
audible "dive-dive-dive" command on a submarine. It
galvanized us into motion, first into the fire pants, then the fire
jacket. I grabbed my helmet and ran to start the fire engine.

I still got excited as when I was a small boy playing with a
toy fire truck. Now, I got to actually drive a real big one.
However, as an adult, my excitement needed to be restrained
because of the real dangers that can happen on a site.

One night the klaxon went off and sped to the Fire Station that was a few blocks from my house. I raced through the procedures to suit up and jump on the fire truck. Adrenaline dumped into my veins.

The dispatcher sent us to the Mill, a regional lumber operation. Already, we had an emotional reaction because the Mill was the economic anchor of our community and its main employer. The name alone, the Mill, flung its one hundred plus years of history at us.

We all knew she was so very old and so very dry. Even from a distance, we could see flames reaching above and around the old girl. I was so high on adrenaline that I have no memory of driving the 20,000 pound fire engine five miles to the site.

When we arrived, I jumped out of the driver's seat and approached the side of the truck to face a panel with a dozen dials and gauges that pushed water out a hose to waiting firefighters at the nozzle end. My brain was so overdosed that I was confused and knowing what to do with the dials became a mystery.

Other firefighters had already stretched the 2 inch line out and braced themselves for the charge of water that had the ability to knock them off their feet. A minute passed. At the truck-end of the fire hose where I stood, staring dumbly at the pressure gauges and dials, I could hear religious words:

"JEEESUS, Pastor!" one yelled, "Gimmie water!"

I threw up my arms in the familiar gesture that clearly signaled that I did not know what I was doing. One of the seasoned firefighters ran back the full length of the fire hose to press the right buttons, turn dials, and pull levers. Water surged into the line.

How did he know which dials to turn? In two minutes, 500 gallons were gone. Then it became clear that we had to go into the Mill itself.

I grabbed a fire axe from the side of the engine and headed into the inferno. It is hard to imagine an inferno until you walk into one. I paired up with a man I greatly respected as a professional firefighter, Gary Bowman.

"Is this the first big fire you have been on?" Gary shouted through his facemask.

"YES!" I yelled back. On this cool night, my hot breath fogged up my face shield.

Gary got right in my face, face-shield to face-shield, and asked a direct question in command form, "Can you stay on my six?" (Slang for "stay on my back.") I nodded "yes."

Once inside, we quickly realized the fires were much more extensive than they appeared to be from the outside. The Mill was a complicated maze of rooms and hallways with fires popping out of the walls and ceilings. Acrid smoke hampered our vision, stinging our eyes and forcing them shut to get relief.

I grabbed the end of my axe to open walls that were releasing smoke plumes. I was making progress when suddenly, I realized that I had made a huge blunder. Distracted by the fires, I got separated from Gary.

"Gary," I yelled. He could not possibly hear me over the tremendous roar of the surrounding fires, groaning timbers and falling debris. My space was fast becoming intolerably hot and was racing toward a flashover. If that came to pass, we could die from burned lungs.

I continued stamping out small fires with my heavy boots, all the while knowing this could end as a personal disaster for several of us. Again, I looked around the room and yelled for Gary. My adrenaline was spent. My heart pounded and I felt panic rising within me.

In front of me, a load-bearing wall belched smoke between seams of old boards. Up to that point, I had been using the pointy pick side of my fireman's axe to pry boards from walls. This wall needed to be torn apart faster.

I flipped the axe head around 180º so as to use the 6 inch blade. This side had a greater striking surface than the pick side. For maximum leverage, I grabbed the far end of the handle and swung it vertically over my head as if I were chopping wood or releasing a Hail Mary pass at the end of a tied football game.

The powerful chopping blow did not land on solid wall, like I expected it should. Instead, the blade easily sliced through the wall as if it were tissue paper. The wall, which had been consumed internally by the fire, dissolved as powdery red cinders before my eyes. Then I caught a horrifying sight.

Gary was standing on the other side in the direct path of my axe.

Unable to stop the momentum of the axe, I watched the razor sharp blade pass through the wall and within an inch of Gary's nose, barely clearing the front of his facemask.

Gary felt the hot swoosh of air as my axe dropped in front of him like a guillotine. Caught off guard at the sudden appearance of an axe coming at him, his stunned eyes popped open and his body instantly recoiled as he instinctively lurched backward.

A fraction of a second later and my axe would have impacted the side of his head. Like a flashbulb from an old Kodak camera, my mind took an instant picture of that moment that takes its turn appearing on the back of my brain.

We had never been more than three feet apart, but the wall was serving as both a visual and a sound barrier. More importantly, I was not "on his six," more like on his three.

© 70189650 / Dollar Photo Club

I fully expected Gary to yell at me for not following him and to order me off the site. He would have been right to do so. Instead, he showed me what a self-controlled professional does under stress. Gary stayed calm and just shook his head, making it clear that he knew how close I had come to killing him.

"Stay on my six," he ordered once more. I stepped through the wall and took my position. This time I kept Gary within arm's reach.

After a disaster a team will usually meet to debrief and discuss Lessons Learned. I had made several mistakes. I did not calm my heart rate when the adrenaline raced through it; I focused on the fires in front of me and my eyes turned into tunnel vision; I did not keep $360°$ situational awareness and lost contact with Gary.

I was dangerously cavalier. I went into the Mill fire way too confident about my abilities and almost killed my partner. I believe the Voice was speaking to me through Gary and that I was ignoring it. The Voice was now using the voices around me to guide and protect me.

In the decades since the Mill fire, Gary married Amy and together they raised three lovely daughters. He is superintendent of the largest Charter school system in California. When I occasionally see Gary, I usually pause... I could have killed him for not listening.

Report 6   9/11: How Many Did We Lose?

Sometimes we reach out in love... only to get manhandled by chaos. We all remember where we were on September 11, 2001. I was Pastor at Kirkpatrick Memorial Presbyterian Church in Ringoes, New Jersey, near New York City. My secretary, Carol, and I heard the news that a plane had gone off course and crashed into the World Trade Center. Among the 20,000 people in the two Towers, 26 of our church members worked among them.

We began to write a list of members who had offices in the Twin Towers, along with their phone numbers. We had not finished this task when we witnessed on TV the second jumbo jet strike the 55th floor of the remaining tower. Just before impact, I recognized the company logo, a pair of red capital A's, on the tail of the plane.

"That's an American Airlines 757", I said.

My mind was pierced with the certainty that this was not a plane off course, but a deliberately orchestrated attack on our country. It was the first time many of us became aware of the consuming hatred of men that led to this atrocity.

Not only did these malevolent enemies demolish the World Trade Center that, to them, represented all of the "evils" of capitalism and America's leadership in the world, but they slaughtered the civilian workers in the Twin Towers and innocent passengers on the hijacked airplanes.

"Carol, we are at war with somebody!" I exclaimed. "Isn't Mike Kurti supposed to be flying today?"

"I think Steve Wonsor is also flying," she replied. Both of these men were jumbo jet pilots for American Airlines and often flew out of Logan Airport in Boston where the terrorists boarded the planes they would hijack on that memorable morning. Later, Mike told me that as the planes taxied and waited in line to take off; his plane was between the two hijacked planes from Logan.

Mike and Steve were not just names on a membership list they were dear friends. I knew their wives and precious children. This was true of the other 26 members on the list Carol and I were calling. I loved these people. We were desperately hoping and praying that each call would yield positive results, but realized that the odds were against it.

"We may have lost several people," I told Carol. She nodded and we continued making our way through the list that seemed unbearably long at the time. Even in separate offices Carol could hear the excited tone of my conversations when I made contact with a member.

However, I felt two reactions stirring inside me: Relief and Dread. Inexpressible relief as we heard that one more member was safe ... and sickening dread that the next call would go unanswered.

At the end of two hours, we knew. Miraculously, none of our members were in their offices when the planes hit that September morning. Some of our members were running late, others had breakfast meetings, car trouble or sick children. One member survived because he and his wife had argued and went to bed angry. The next morning, he insisted on the two of them going out to breakfast.

Sadly though, each of them had friends and co-workers who were not late; who did not go to breakfast; who did not have anything delaying their prompt arrival. Though our members survived, they had many funerals to attend and deaths to grieve.

The night before the terrorists' mass murder and destruction, a married couple in our membership attended a small group Bible Study at the home of Todd and Lisa Beamer. You may remember him. He was the brave passenger on Flight 93 who immortalized the phrase, "Let's roll!"

He and other courageous souls prevented that plane from crashing into yet another icon of our culture or population area, all the while knowing that their personal outcome would most likely be death. That proved to be true. Those aboard caused the plane to crash into a vacant field in Pennsylvania. Todd Beamer was a wonderful Christian man, husband, and father of three little boys.

Before the day of September 11th began, I had planned several meetings with groups and appointments with people. I was prepared and ready to make progress on several goals. Again, I assumed I was in control of my day. My calendar looked full and promised to be a productive day. Having control over my calendar gives me the feeling that I am in control of my life and I felt good about the day.

The very nature of a disaster is that our normalcy is disrupted. A disaster means that someone else or something else has taken control away from us. Too often I get sucked into the notion that I am the master of my fate and needed to be the captain of my soul.

My busy calendar reassures me that I am in control of my time. It is a feel-good illusion. However, disasters say otherwise by running over my plans. Dictated by the urgent and manipulated by crises, I try to keep in touch with my soul.

Everything changed for me after 9/11. Because our church was so close to New York City, my precious congregation released me to assist in the recovery effort. The Church saw me as their representative at Ground Zero who could minister where they could not.

For the next nine months, I volunteered at the Family Assistance Center counseling families and at Ground Zero talking with and praying a blessing on police officers, firefighters and steel workers. I would still preach on Sunday mornings but was free from regular duties during the week. Those months changed my life as I began the journey of serving as a Disaster Pastor.

Report 7   Beginnings of a Disaster Pastor

On the evening of September 12, 2001, I reported to the Family Assistance Center (FAC) in the Armory on the Hudson River. This huge facility was larger than a football field and designated as the place for family members and friends to look for lost loved ones.

To assist the surviving families, hundreds of representatives from scores of governmental agencies, relief workers and social service agencies assembled to help. Getting these resources organized was an enormous task. Mindi Russell, who was recruited as the Lead Chaplain, was in one of the only planes in the sky, flying in from Sacramento, California. She was not only my Supervisor at the Family Assistance Center, but has become a good, trusted friend.

As families made their way through the myriad of agencies, they would eventually gather in the spacious food court to rest, eat, and talk. There was an abundance of food on long tables, a seemingly endless supply of tasty hot meals, meandering bowls of fruit and salad items, countless deserts and snacks, all never appearing to become depleted or untended.

Several empty tables surrounded by empty chairs invited families to sit and eat their food. It was a respite place for weary families. Food somehow makes it easier for people to communicate, to recount, to explain or to lament. Food gives us something to do with our hands, something to look at and fuss with when we need to break eye contact.

Families appeared as a cluster of quiet people sitting around a table, not yet sure what they wanted to do or what they should be doing. Being the man with the clergy collar and a banana, I appeared safe, approachable: the Chaplain/Padre. This is where I would innocuously join a family at a table.

I would ask permission to join them and after I was seated, I would begin peeling a banana. I typically began to engage them with an easy-to-answer fact question, "Are you missing a loved one?"

And, they began to tell me their stories. Without ever asking, all they actually wanted to hear me say was, "I can bring your loved one back." They were desperate for someone, especially a Pastor, Priest, Rabbi or Chaplain, to help them awaken from this nightmare.

As a Chaplain, I was asked to listen, absorb, offer prayer and provide comfort. In the six weeks I spent at the Family Assistance Center, not one missing person was found. In retrospect, I discovered that not knowing the details of lost

family members leaves a haunting sense of void. The losses
were magnified by the knowledge that it was an evil,
coordinated attack that stole our innocence. In my forty-plus
years in the ministry, I have never witnessed this level of pain
and heartache.

Eventually I heard hundreds of stories, all painful. Here are
a few I heard one night.

Report 8   Running or Helping

One middle-aged man told me he was sitting at his desk, enjoying a cup of coffee when he noticed a lone jumbo jet off course some distance away. Flight patterns for the three regional airports are rigid, so stray aircraft would be easily spotted.

He saw the plane headed in his direction, growing in size as it got closer and closer. He could see the engines, the pilot, and just before impact, he saw the wings tilting for maximum destructive impact. Miraculously, his office was not hit, but the floor above was.

All hell broke loose at impact. His officemate, a gentleman from India, was flung under a heavy filing cabinet. "Do I escape or help him?" he asked himself. The room was on fire and debris fell everywhere as he pulled the cabinet off his co-worker and both made their way to the ground floor.

When he spoke with me, he wanted help in dealing with the consuming anger he felt whenever he saw anyone he perceived as Arab. I found that to be a common reaction that many people had to deal with in the days, weeks, and months following 9/11.

Newlywed/Widow

An attractive woman in her late thirties screamed and
wailed over the loss of her husband of less than one year. He
was a trader for a Wall Street firm.

"How could people do these evil things and kill so many
innocent people?" She screamed loud enough for everyone to
hear and move away. I did not try to stop her. Each minute her
loud sobs explored the extremes of suffering and despair rarely
visited by human beings. Minute after minute her wails and
cries came in waves. Some cries had tones of anger that
alternated with cries of woeful loss. I just sat with her, banana
in hand, and listened.

The scriptures tell us to "weep with those who weep."[7]
While I am not emotionally equipped to go to her depth of pain,
I was still able to give her comfort and acceptance. Tears
flooded her swollen eyes and her convulsing body begged for
answers I did not have. More minutes passed. Eventually she
ran out of tears and out of energy for crying. Spent and
exhausted, she sat contemplating her loss.

"Do you have someone who can take you home?" I asked.
After I asked, I realized she drove here on her own. She nodded
her head, reached into her large purse and dialed a friend.

---

[7] Romans 12.15

Immigrants

Undocumented workers told me in hushed tones that they were good enough to vacuum floors, empty trash and clean toilets, but were not good enough to receive benefits from the Victim Compensation Fund. Some believed that if they put in a claim, they would be deported back to Mexico. These family members impacted me greatly. Their vulnerability was heart-wrenching. Each time, I prayed that God would give them wisdom and opportunity for justice.

Sisters

I grabbed another banana and found two women sitting at a table with a toddler boy in between them. They were two sisters who were missing a loved one, their oldest sister, Louisa. On that Tuesday morning of September 11th, Louisa called one of her sisters to report she was safe and leaving her office. A moment later she called right back later saying, "I forgot my purse."

"It will only take a minute," she reported, confidently. That minute became the bridge between life and death, the space where death is the inadvertent choice. Louisa left behind a five-year old son.

But, there was something different about the two surviving sisters sitting before me. They, along with the missing third sister, were Christians, safe and at peace in their belief in Jesus Christ.

"We lost our sister, and this small boy lost his mom, but we know that one day we will be with her again in heaven. We are just as devastated as everyone here, but we have hope." Their faith ministered to me. Faith gave them a hope to make their grieving bearable.

Brothers

"Have you seen our brother?" asked one of three brothers searching for the fourth. They were desperate and standing by one of the many walls plastered with pictures of missing loved ones. They had flyers with his picture and contact information.

Their brother had attended a one-hour job interview at Windows on the World, a restaurant on the top of the North Tower on floors 106 and 107. He was on the 107th floor when the plane struck.

I thought to myself that they have not found anybody who was in that restaurant, nor anyone from 25 floors below. There was a great deal of anxiety in these brothers' eyes, anxiety that revealed their state of denial, as if their brother were only lost and their job was to find where he was. In reality, he was already dead.

I Got Out, But . . .

Melissa, twenty-eight years old, was an office manager who
called her father from her cell phone to share the joyous news
that she "just got out of the Tower!" She was coming home,
she said. She never arrived. Falling debris rained down on her,
taking her life.

Melissa's father had hope based on the information his
daughter had given him. When I talked to him, I realized that in
this case, hope did not change stark reality. That telling
someone to just have positive thoughts is not always based in
reality and may feel like a betrayal later.

The Firefighter

Next was the wife of a young firefighter. She showed me his picture. As others fled the looming infernos, her husband, the father of their four young boys, put aside the natural instinct to save himself and instead, followed his training and ran into the building.

Fitzroy

"Do you have a missing loved one?" This can be a fruitful starter question and only requires a yes or no answer. With a fresh banana, I approached a table with a man who was visiting his son in New York City. He was from The Commonwealth of Dominica, a tiny island nation in the Caribbean. There are barely 71,000 inhabitants and I imagine this trip to New York

City, the heartbeat of the financial world, was a dream come true for him.

He appeared to be about my age and I deeply regret that I do not know his name. He began to tell me about his son, Fitzroy, who worked in the Twin Towers repairing switchboards and telephone lines. His face began to beam. He was obviously proud of his son for landing such a lucrative and prestigious job in America. On Tuesday morning, he received a call from Fitzroy, who was working on the eighty-sixth floor.

"Dad! Turn on the TV and tell me what happened!" Fitzroy felt the building shake, but had no notion of what had happened. The father stopped speaking, removed his billfold and dug out a photograph of his son, then continued telling me his story.

The snapshot showed a handsome young man, smiling confidently into the lens as if the world were his oyster and all he had to do was follow the path he had set out for himself.

"I turned on the TV and told him a plane had hit his Tower," the father remarked, "I started shaking and screaming, 'Get out, son, get out!'"

"I tried, Dad," yelled his desperate son, the fear and panic racing through the phone like a manic missile. "There's smoke in the hallway." Speaking as fast as he could, he explained that he was trapped by flames spreading from the lower floors and that the stairwell had collapsed.

"Dad, I'm in trouble. Fire is in the room." His voice became calmer, softer as he made his final comments. "I love you and Mom and the family. Dad, I can't make it out. I love you." The conversation suddenly ended, the line went dead. His father, standing motionless like a statue, watched the TV screen as the Tower fell.

I pictured my son and myself in his situation. That is never a good idea because now his story became my story. The heat shield protecting the tender parts inside me was breached. Though second hand, his trauma became mine.

As I listened, my throat began to close up in anticipation of the tears I would stifle, and I experienced that familiar punch in the gut that always accompanies human suffering. This soft-spoken man continued, as if talking about Fitzroy helped establish the memory of him.

"Fitzroy came to America to get a good job and to send money home so his six brothers and sisters could go to college. It was my son's hope that after all of his younger siblings finished with their education, then he would marry and start a family of his own."

He was pleased with his boy's achievements and pride shone through his grief-filled face. His eyes were red and swollen, filled with exhaustion, as he told me that Fitzroy raised money twice a year to sponsor mission trips by The Exodus Team to his home country, Dominica. This sad, gentle man was well pleased with the sacrificial character of his child.

I was unprepared for the sheer volume of human suffering and for the desperate sorrow. I found myself listening to a horrific story every 30 minutes for up to twelve hours at a time.

Now, I hate bananas.

Report 9   Listening Can Be Damaging

The other chaplains and I would meet regularly to discuss the most horrible, difficult cases in hopes of off-loading them. It was a mandatory debriefing. We met in private to prevent shards of atrocities from inadvertently landing on the already dismantled psyches around us. Six or eight of us sat on folding chairs in a circle. Among us were no superstars with giant churches, just local pastors, regular priests and caring rabbis.

Our routine amounted to four hours with victims, a half-hour with my fellow chaplains to debrief, then back to the victims and families for another four hours. Listening to the non-stop emotional hammering and stomping, packed down the soft, fertile soil of my soul.

The purpose of the debrief sessions with the chaplains was meant to help defuse and off-load the worst of the stories. For me, it did not. I only heard the worst of the worst of their stories. After attending a couple of these sessions, I could no longer bear hearing more trauma of everyone's most toxic stories.

I entered one of the six stalls and locked the door. This tiny space became my sanctuary, my refuge, a hiding place. I regretted my inability to stay the course with my colleagues, but I knew I was past my limits!

After thirty minutes, when other chaplains finished the debrief, they entered the restroom before resuming their duties. The debrief session was finally over and I could exit my cell of safety. One of the chaplains had noticed my absence and commented on it.

"We missed you at the last debrief. Are you okay?"

"Yeah, I got a phone call from Mother Nature," I quipped.

He did not respond, but during the next chaplain debrief meeting when I retreated to the men's room, not a minute had passed when he followed me and checked into the sanctuary cell next to mine, locking the door behind him.

"Toby, are you in here?" came his voice from the next stall.

"Yep," I replied. "Why are you in here?"

"I just couldn't listen to the stories anymore," he said quietly.

"I couldn't either," I said. We sat in silence and a minute later, a third chaplain followed our lead. Eventually, chaplains occupied all of the stalls.

The accumulation of stories that I call "Dark Knowledge" overwhelmed my natural strengths and reserves. I was so emotionally spent, as well as mentally and physically exhausted, that I was not safe anymore. I feared I would say something stupid, reckless, or thoughtless. I did not want to inflict my stress on these vulnerable people.

I suppose that I could have taken breaks during those nine months in other pursuits, like returning to being a regular pastor at my church. But I found my calling to be a Disaster Pastor, to be someone safe for people who needed to begin their grieving process by telling their stories.

I could not abandon these dear people. I determined to steel my insides and continue. I was on the edge, at risk, but I had to go back one more time. The next night hundreds of people sat in the food court of the FAC, waiting and needing to tell me their Human Cry. Something clicked inside me.

I realized, "I cannot do this anymore."

I had been ignoring the small Voice inside of me, challenging me to stop responding to the messianic urge to help everyone. Finally, I could no longer ignore my extreme level of internal pain; I could not handle the crush of hearing so many aching stories day after day and week after week.

Intent on bringing hope to the broken-hearted, I felt like I was living in hell. Trying to bring peace and calm to others, I now did not have it myself. The human mind was not wired to stay in soul-extremis longer than necessary, at least mine was not.

I needed to give the people at the FAC to the Lord and trust that God would help them by sending others in my place. For the first time I asked for help. I asked our gifted Lead Chaplain, Mindi Russell, to reassign me to Ground Zero.

I admit that I was emotionally ill-equipped for the intensity of my interactions with family members and friends. Over time I learned to listen to people's pain without absorbing their trauma. They could off-load their story onto me without me picking it up. The burdened they carried did not have to become mine.

Report 10   To Ground Zero

Exiting the Family Assistance Center, I made my way past multiple layers of military and police checkpoints and averted my eyes from the waves of people crying out for my help.

This night, I was refreshed by the cool night air and sucked it in by the gulping mouthfuls. I walked down to Ground Zero and passed the Wall of the Missing. I looked at a few of the hundreds of pictures attached to this wall alongside St. Paul's Chapel. After many months of passing by those pictures, some of the Missing began to look like people I knew.

One face stood out among the others on the Wall. It was an African-American pastor. His picture kept intruding in my mind. My exterior appeared fine, but I was off-balance inside. I had been at the World Trade Center numerous times on a Tuesday. Why was that pastor's face on the Wall and not mine?

On this, my first entry into Ground Zero, I was ushered to an equipment room to don a breathing mask, moon suit and hardhat. I recall thinking that the moon suit perfectly complemented the surreal landscape, which made me smile.

Without the hazmat protection, the smells of acrid plastic, toxic fumes and burnt flesh wrenched the stomach. The respirator helped filter the toxins but not the stench.

Does this look safe to breath?

I stepped out of the equipment room and ventured onto the Pile with the construction workers and First Responders. There were several monikers for Ground Zero including The Pit, The Site, The Pile, and perhaps more that I did not hear.

As I worked there for the remainder of the nine months, I favored the name "The Pit," but with the passage of time, Ground Zero has trumped all other names.

One night, I had been making my way around Ground Zero and dropped into one of the five Salvation Army warming stations spread around the perimeter of The Pile. Each of these command-size tents could easily seat fifty people, and lining the inside walls were large bins with new, heavy-duty work gloves, boots, winter coats, helmets and safety glasses for the workers. For free! A nurse was on duty to administer first aid to torn fingers and countless other minor injuries.

As winter crept in, the snow fell and the nights grew bitter cold. What a relief to feel the warmth of the gas-fired heaters behind cheerful faces of volunteers who greeted me, each one eager to help. I approached a table whose smells and gourmet offerings beckoned to me.

The large pots of hot chocolate with whipped cream and marshmallows sat alongside cauldrons of hot coffee with every imaginable flavored creamer – the small comforts that let all of us know that these kind folks recognized our longing for anything close to normalcy.

The Salvation Army helped keep nearby restaurants on their feet financially by buying food at a fair price and then turning around and serving it at no cost to the workers at Ground Zero. I was unaware that this was how Salvation Army worked.

I was pleasantly surprised to discover that death or injury was not a requirement to receive aid from them. Warmed, rested and refueled, I left this haven and resumed my trek to interact with and pray a blessing on people at the Pile.

Well past midnight, I saw a man who appeared to be directing the activities of numerous steel workers. A steady stream of men walked up to him, spoke briefly, and walked away. In between moments when he was not conversing with a worker, he gave orders through his radio.

Even from a distance, I could tell he was the go-to man, the Superintendent. Clearly he was surprised to see a clergyman meandering among his workers.

"Good evening, Father," he called. I learned that indeed, he was the Superintendent of the thousand steel workers at the site – 1,000 steel workers!

A solitary figure, he was similar to the Supreme Allied Commander at Ground Zero, or just like a conductor of an orchestra, he controlled all movement, issued all directions. I knew I had less than a minute, so I jumped to the question I asked most of his workers.

"What would you like the Lord to do for you?" It was like flipping a switch. His face twisted into a torrent of emotion a fraction of a second before he spoke.

"You know what really makes me mad?" he yelled and waved his arms. I just stood there assuming he was going to complain about my presence or something. "My workers are freezing their butts off because we aren't allowed in the Red Cross warming tent!"

Here was a man obviously accustomed to being in control of his surroundings. However, the weather was not cooperating; he was furious that the snow and biting cold would not bend to his will. He could not do anything about that.

Worse, his workers were not permitted to enter the Red Cross warming tents and there was nothing he could do about that, either.

From my perspective, this restriction was a misguided decision that limited relief aid only for police, firefighters and city employees, but not civilian workers. It was obvious that this Super cared deeply about those who worked for him. He reluctantly accepted what the weather did, but not the exclusion of his freezing men from food and warmth. He was justifiably angry.

"Is there anything you can do?" he asked.

"Yes," I said confidently. Without permission or authority, I announced, "Send them to the Salvation Army's warming tents." I pointed in the direction of the nearest one.

His eyes lit up. "Seriously?"

"They'll take care of your guys," I promised.

He turned away, raised his radio, pressing the talk button on an open channel, and said, "Everybody, listen up." There was no need to identify himself, his voice was recognizable to everyone.

"When you take your breaks, go to the Salvation Army tents. They will take care of you." Turning back to me he said, "This is an answer to prayer. I am grateful." The one-minute conversation ended as a worker approached his boss.

"What have I done?" I thought to myself. I just made a promise I had no permission to make.

© Salvation Army

Only a couple of weeks earlier, a Salvation Army Major had told me, "The five stations we run at Ground Zero cost about $110,000.00 per week." All funding came from volunteer donations.

Without their knowledge or consent, I had easily doubled their costs. Now, the most responsible thing I had to do was tell someone at the Salvation Army the outrageous promise I just made.

I walked a few steps towards the nearest Salvation Army tent, still a hundred feet away, when a Salvation Army Officer approached me wearing his easily recognizable uniform. We greeted each other.

I was very surprised to see him because I never saw a Salvation Army Officer on The Pile before this moment and would not see one again. They always stayed in the tents giving aid to the workers. Tonight, however, God arranged a special meeting to rescue me from my fast-lips affliction.

"Uh," I stammered, "I need to tell you what I just obligated your organization to do." I explained what I promised the Superintendent just a minute before. I was prepared for him to rebuke me for my reckless pledge.

"Send them all to us," he said, without hesitation. "We'll take care of them." Those were the same words I told the Superintendent.

I closed my eyes for one second and sighed, "Thank you Lord". When I opened my eyes the Officer was gone. He could not have run away; I would have seen him. Rather, he just disappeared. That may sound hard to believe, but he was gone. An angel? Maybe. But he sure did look like a Salvation Army Officer.

I cannot offer enough praise for the Salvation Army for doing what all of the rescue agencies could and should have done. Their policy was to help anyone who walked in their tents. Since then I have relied on the Salvation Army when I need to connect people with those who have the resources.

It has always been a mystery how God arranges the connections, and I never tire of watching it happen. The conversations with the Superintendent and the Salvation Army Officer captured a spiritual reality that I experienced repeatedly at Ground Zero: Divine Appointments.

Divine Appointments happen almost every day of my life. Each morning, I ask God to arrange Divine Appointments with people needing help. When those meetings occur I sense God's presence doing a special work between us.

Trusting that Divine Appointments will happen gives me confidence to enter into big problems and believe that God will show up. I am so certain of God's purpose for my life that I plunge into dark situations with my little light and find time and again a steady stream of Divine Appointments.

Every time things have worked out, gone right, ended well, I know that it was due to God and not "good luck" or any skills I might have. My daily routine is to move from one Divine Appointment to the next.

Report 11   Listening Past Limits

The hour-long train ride home provided a transition time between the Family Assistance Center or The Pit and home, fleeing hell for what felt very close to heaven – my cozy church parsonage in a beautiful flora-laden county in New Jersey.

I needed to get back with people who watched football on TV, who invited us to their barbeques, who loved me and whose kids chased fireflies at night. I needed to get back among the living.

All I could think about was getting back to my wife, Judy, to debrief with her and attempt to release the recorded voices from within. I am proficient in recreating an event or conversation verbatim, so all that was missing for her were the sights and sounds of big machines, toxic smells and the occasional belch of fire coming out of the ground.

It did not occur to me that I might be overwhelming her like I had already done to myself. Hopefully, retelling her what happened through second-hand did not stomp on fertile areas in her innocent mind or gentle heart. Actually, Judy appreciated me sharing my stories, experiences and reactions with her without becoming overwhelmed.

Judy loves to hear my thoughts and what is happening in my life. So, every night, she was eager to hear the stories and watch my face and body language as I unloaded.

My wife is a gifted counselor and was my lifeline each evening when I left the Family Assistance Center and Ground Zero. Every night, just as I did with the broken-hearted, she started with a fact-based question to ease me into the vocal release.

Often, as I lay in bed for hours, I could not sleep. Of course, some nights when I did sleep, the surreal dream images were worse than no sleep at all. Even if I were to get ten hours of sleep, it could not peel off the layers of horror I had heard and seen the night before.

My frustration at not being able to effectively restore those who were devastated by their great loss grew as the days crept forward. What could I realistically give them?

There were no tidy, prepackaged answers to eternal questions and no satisfying platitudes. The only thing I could give was to listen with care to their Human Cry and pray a blessing on them.

I found myself beginning to understand survivors' guilt and developed a keen empathy for what our soldiers suffer when they return home from combat.

I took a look at what I had been doing at Ground Zero and how it was affecting both my congregation and me. Reluctantly, I decided to scale back to every other night so I could rest, regain my equilibrium and return to ministering to my church.

Report 12   Ceremonies In The Pit

Ground Zero was certainly a dangerous place to serve with its multiple possibilities of becoming severely injured or contaminated. Fires beneath the piles would suddenly belch out smoke and flames like an angry dragon coming awake at unscheduled intervals.

Several times the blaze shot through the spot where I had just been standing. The Pile looked especially hellish at night. When winter arrived with falling snow, the ground was still hot but the air was bitter cold, sending up steamy, foggy clouds that seemed ghostly, like the scenes in an old black and white movie set in London in the winter.

The incessant gnawing and gnashing of huge earth movers and diggers became a type of white noise, although with extremely high decibels. They never stopped, unless it was to change crane operators or when a body was recovered.

The huge machines looked like some sort of prehistoric monsters, taking large bites of steel and concrete so as to open up dangerous passageways for the rescue workers to descend a little deeper into The Pit.

When a body of a police officer or firefighter was retrieved, a whistle blew three times and all work ceased. All work. The cranes and backhoes lowered their buckets and the machines appeared to be in an attitude of prayer with heads bowed, waiting for the recovery rituals to begin. A rescue carrier would be taken to the location of the body, which was then carefully placed in the basket.

An American flag was reverently draped across the basket, covering the body. Firefighters would take the four corners of the basket and slowly make their way between long lines of workers that had spontaneously formed to the waiting ambulance 300 feet away at the top of The Pit.

Workers took off their hard hats, civilians placed their right hand over their hearts and police officers saluted at attention. Unlike a funeral service in a church, there were no words, no music or choirs singing. Silence penetrated the whole area. We were on holy ground. These moments were sacred. A Divine Appointment was visiting us.

© SteveSpak.com

Hundreds quickly formed two long lines and stood shoulder to shoulder to form a path for the litter bearers to carry the victim. Workers initiated these solemn lines themselves, each of us felt compelled to participate in a sacred event.

Steel workers turned off their blowtorches, crane operators left their machines and fire fighters stopped their recovery efforts. The collective decibels dropped from 100+ to a holy silence.

It did not require a pastor to suggest what should be done or how to organize what happened – it was innately within their souls to honor and respect the dead.

Some would reach out to the flag or basket as if by touching, they were sending prayers to heaven, notifying the Lord that another one was on the way. Others would salute or make the sign of the cross, all acknowledging a life lived and lost.

While standing in the ceremonial lines on a dozen different nights, I wept until I had no more tears; we all wept.

We have a deep human need to turn the recovery of a dead body, even at a noisy construction site, into a sacred ceremony. It was symbolic of the values of our culture that bodies are important and not to be discarded or left behind.

These ceremonies were holy moments.

Disaster work is a terrible-honor.

Report 13   Theology in The Pit

In the previous report, I wrote about the Divine Appointments, those special meetings that only God can arrange. There was a second spiritual reality: Divine Moments.

God-moments are when people speak of deeply important matters, heart to heart, soul to soul, and sometimes, tears to tears. During these moments the other person and I were joined by the unseen Voice in a three-way conversation that ministered to our soul and spirit. While standing in small pockets between twisted I-beams, God's presence surrounded our bodies and filled our conversation with grace.

Ground Zero was an intensely holy, spiritual place, in part because so many people had died there. Like Gettysburg, it evoked enormous pain while commanding reverence from the folks who were working there.

The combination made for a deeply spiritual setting. It reminded me of a tight cluster of giant Redwood trees that formed a natural chapel at their center. One could shout if they wished but the setting stimulated a sense of awe, where whispering felt right. At Ground Zero, even amidst the constant roar of machines, God Moments occurred with each cluster of workers huddled just around the next pile of discarded I-beams.

Hundreds of times, the police, firefighters and steel workers wondered aloud with me why a loving, omnipotent, omniscient, transcendent God would allow such evil to occur. We pondered the mystery of an All Powerful God versus Free Will... to no conclusions.

These workers had seen and experienced firsthand what our minds could not comprehend. The Why question always came up. Usually, I listened for their Human Cry and prayed with them.

At Ground Zero, a typical conversation was with Mike, an NYFD firefighter. His God-moment occurred during a 12-hour shift of sifting through rubble searching for survivors, in what we all came to know was a fruitless endeavor. He was experiencing an in-your-face anger over his friends' deaths and longed to see and talk with them again.

"Pray for me," he pleaded, "to re-connect with God. I haven't been in church for a long time, but I am a believer."

I spoke with NYPD Officer Richard, who entered a deli across from Ground Zero to clear his lungs, catch his breath and escape the dust. "I'm not religious but I am spiritual," he said. I prayed for his safety and that he would feel the hand of God on him. After a couple of minutes, he went back into the chaos.

These requests for prayer and blessings came again and again from workers who barely had time to stop for food and nature breaks. However, they took a moment to receive a blessing from me and assure them that God was already there with them.

"The Hand of God is on you," I said hundreds of times.

I wish I could recall the names of each of these courageous workers who seemed to sense that I genuinely cared about them and was concerned for them. As I listened, they shared more and more parts of their stories. I sensed that my empathy helped relieve them of burdens that ached to be shared and understood. Talking seemed to help siphon some of the deep sorrow away from their trauma.

Each night, my routine became settled into a seven-hour circuit around the perimeter of Ground Zero. I would approach small groups of firefighters, policemen or steel workers. Frequently they would approach me. I always started with a fact question like, "How long have you been on your feet?"

Someone in the cluster would make a comment or ask a question. Sometimes I would ask them, "So, what do you make of this?" Everyone had an answer or opinion. I would just listen and a God-moment would surely follow.

After working a few months on The Pile, I noticed that other chaplains were conspicuously absent. I assumed they quit volunteering when the initial excitement had turned into hard work. I was disappointed.

Unbeknownst to me, after about three months the Red Cross had banned all chaplains from working at Ground Zero because of the danger of injury or death from the operations of the monstrous equipment and the spontaneous bursts of fire that belched from the inferno below.

The badge I wore that gave me privileged access to Ground Zero had a three-month time limit. As the third expiration approached, I had to renew my badge to continue working at Ground Zero.

Just before the ninth month, when I met with the Red Cross, they were visibly horrified to learn that I had continued making my rounds at The Pit. They accused me of "self-deploying" and called me a "rogue chaplain" for not complying with the ban. I was stunned.

Then, I realized that the ban explained why the other chaplains had suddenly disappeared. However, despite having given the Red Cross my schedule and all of my contact information, they never informed me to stop working. It appears that I was the only chaplain that served at Ground Zero for the entire nine months.

I am thrilled that I did not know about the ban on chaplains. It allowed me to minister to hundreds of the greatest first responders.

Report 14   His Last 15 Minutes

I go to disasters with various teams, including one whose specialty is serving in high-risk medical events. This team has a unique and reoccurring challenge.

They need to manage their extremely high frustration levels while functioning in sub-standard conditions with none of the high tech tools they are accustomed to using in their work back home. And there is a special guilt associated with not doing all you know you could have done if only you had access to the high tech resources back home.

It is commonly assumed that the Hippocratic Oath[8] directs physicians to "Do no harm." It is not mandatory that all new physicians take this oath, but those who do, take it freely.

The Oath has a hidden assumption - namely, that the doctor will have the best resources available so as to choose the best practices in the treatment of their patients. However, in austere disaster settings, that oath becomes superseded with a new ethic: "Do what you can with what you have... as fast as you can."

---

[8] The Hippocratic oath: text, translation and interpretation By Ludwig Edelstein Page 56 ISBN 978-0-8018-0184-6 (1943) . A copy of the modern versions of the Hippocratic Oath can be retrieved at http://en.wikipedia.org/wiki/Hippocratic_Oath

One surgeon I highly respect walked me through this concept. He told me about a young girl who was rescued from her burning home and rushed to his emergency room with third-degree burns over 99% of her body.

"It is rare to survive a 40% burn," he began, "so I understood right away how critical this girl was when she arrived." He explained that skin is the largest organ of the body and protects us against pathogens and excessive water loss. With most of the skin burned away, there is nothing standing between the ravaged body and infection.

"What did you do?" I asked.

"We gave her 20mg of morphine," he answered.

"Really? You killed her?" I asked, incredulous at this last statement.

"We ended her suffering," he gently replied. "She was going to die regardless of anything we did, but only after slow, agonizing hours of extreme pain, followed by certain death."

"You did a mercy killing?" I asked. As I type this now, I cringe at how accusatory my question must have sounded.

"No. It was mercy," he simply replied.

"Hmm," I pondered. My surgeon friend does not consider himself a follower of Christ, but even so, I heard the Voice speak through him to give me this special message.

It is common for my teammates to feel guilty when they talk about the "do what you have to do" decisions, knowing they could have saved more lives if only we were back at their modern medical facility... if only we had adequate supplies... if only we had anesthesia when we were tasked with severing limbs....

In austere places we do not have high tech equipment or life-saving supplies of medicines. We have to suspend our high tech mind-set and practices for primitive high touch methods. Even with our best efforts, people die.

When we arrived at one site, medical personnel summoned me to the Black Tag Room, a euphemism for the Morgue. I entered the room to see three medical personnel hovering over a slender man lying on a pallet two inches off the concrete floor. As they looked up to acknowledge me, my clergy collar was all the information they needed to transfer this patient's care to me.

"His name is Arzil," one of the medical staff said. "He came in with a bullet wound to his abdomen." I was surprised to learn the man was twenty-five; he appeared to be at least forty-five. It was obvious that he had done a lot of hard living from the looks of the scars and marks on him. His rugged, tough body was relaxed now, giving no indication of what life may have held for him.

"He is dying," another staff member added. The three of them stepped back and huddled together to discuss another case. Kneeling beside Arzil's head was a civilian couple. With their hand they motioned me to join them.

"We are Christians and believe in prayer," they stated. I sat down cross-legged at Arzil's head. The husband asked me to pray. I felt awkward.

They looked at me as if I were on stage and I felt that they were listening for evidence that I was really a Christian. One of the medical staff watched to see how I would perform. I was on display, acutely aware that I was auditioning for them.

One the other hand, sometimes people believe that because I am a Pastor, my prayers are more likely to get noticed by God and answered. Some people seem to think that my prayers are treated as Priority Mail.

I guess it is natural to "go to the pro," but it has always bothered me to be set up higher than anyone else who prays to the same God. After all, it is God who answers and heals, not me.

Generally, prayers get answered in God's timing as the Spirit of God works in and through us. Some people have a boat load of faith, some have a small amount the size of a tiny seed. Somehow the prayers get sorted and answered. "Lord," I began, "heal Arzil. Amen."

That was probably too short and direct for their liking. The couple got up and drifted away. I do not know if they were disappointed by my quickie prayer or if they just needed a break from the intense atmosphere – the sounds, smells, sights all combined to make any of us want to turn on our heels and escape from this awful room of death and dying.

I stayed with Arzil, pulling him further into my lap. Although his build was slight, his added weight on my crossed legs made me keenly aware of the concrete floor. Even in the heat, the cold seeped through to my hip joints and they screamed with pain. My sitting position threatened more torture if I did not move and relieve my joints.

"Lord, I don't know if this man is a believer," I prayed softly. Alone, I felt more comfortable praying and leaned closely into him, speaking with a soft voice into his ear, "Arzil, can you hear me?" There was no facial movement or any other acknowledgement that he heard me.

I can usually discern if my prayer will be answered or not. This time, I knew it would be "not." I do not know how I know, I just do. His eyelids were crusty and only half-open; his breathing was slow and very shallow.

Every breath moved him closer to the end of his life. Reaching forward for his left hand that limply rested on his abdomen, I could feel that his fingers were stiff and cold. Though still breathing, rigor was creeping up his body.

How did he get shot, I wondered? What was happening when the trigger was pulled? Did a police officer shoot him or was it a gang-banger? I had an instant picture in my mind of a bullet screaming through his flesh and realized that it did not matter who actually pulled the trigger... the result was the same.

It most certainly would not have been anyone's first choice to spend his or her last minutes of life cradled in a stranger's lap. I stopped musing and admitted that I would not likely discover answers to any of my questions about Arzil. So, I sat quietly with him, waiting.

"Lord, if You are not going to heal Arzil, then bring him to Yourself." Continuing to hold him, I felt his life slipping away.

I wished his family could have been sitting here with him, holding him and saying their goodbyes. Would they ever know what had happened to him? Would they wonder if he were washed out to sea or got buried by the mud? Had they thought that Arzil had been evacuated to one of the host cities? There would be little chance his family would learn what happened.

"Does he have friends or family here?" I asked a nearby medic. He shook his head no. If he did not know, then how was he brought here? I turned back to look into Arzil's eyes. Arzil was spending his last 15 minutes of his life with me. It was sobering to me because it was a sacred moment on holy ground.

With virtually no equipment, the medical staff moved to the next patient, scrambling to help the ones with even a slim chance of living. The next patient was Carlos. A little later he, too, died in my arms.

There would be more occasions where I pulled the dying into my lap to comfort them during their last fifteen minutes. Each time I look into their eyes, I knew that I was looking into my own future, the hereafter. I wondered where I would spend the last 15 minutes of my life... and with whom.

Report 15   Divine Appointment with Fear

We took off on a regional commuter jet from North Carolina on a one-hour flight to Alabama after a town, Tuscaloosa, was ravaged by a Category 5 hurricane. Halfway through the flight, I heard the starboard engine change pitch and wind down.

The pitch change would be a normal sound if the pilot were beginning a landing approach, which he did not appear to be doing. There should be no reason for this to happen when the plane reaches its cruising altitude. Passengers around me did not seem to notice the change in pitch.

The pilot came on the intercom. His rumbling voice sounded like the very voice of God.

"Ladies and gentlemen, our instruments indicate a significant drop in oil pressure in one engine." He did not alarm the passengers with the rest of the story, which was, "the engine is completely dead!"

This large plane packed with sleepy people was suspended in the air by one engine. People immediately became alert, sat up straight and spoke with one another. I had an immediate reaction. It was a strange thought aimed directly to God.

"Lord, if you want to have me die this day, you do not have to kill the other 80 people on this plane." I felt the fear rising inside, trying to do its job.

Fear has a pure motive. Its only purpose is to protect us… by warning us of danger. After it alerts us, it has done its job and then needs to be managed and controlled. It may not sound very spiritual on my part, but I can carry a full measure of faith in my heart and an equal amount of fear in my head.

Fear can be contagious.

My seatmate was a middle-aged woman who had closed her eyes immediately upon boarding, the universal signal that no conversation was desired. Now her eyes were wide open.

"What's happening?," she blurted out fearfully.

"The pilot said there is a small problem with the engine outside our window." I almost felt proud of my restraint. I reassured her, "Just to be safe, he is returning to the airport." If fear took over I might have screamed, "That engine mounted four feet from our seats is dead. We are going to die! Die! DIE!"

I purposely try to keep my fears that cannot be calmed at a distance while at the same time govern my anxieties that cannot be fully controlled internally.

In my role as Disaster Pastor I try to manage my fear and anxiety with preferred responses of logic, reason and empathy in order to be part of the solution. Specifically, I have a conversation with my fears.

"Fear," I will begin, "thank you for alerting me to this danger." I am acknowledging this strong emotion whose intent is to make sure I suffer no harm. "You have done your job. You can relax. I will take it from here." With that self-talk my insides relax and my mind is free to use its energy to find a solution.

"Are we going to crash?" she asked, quickly looking around to assess the moods of the other passengers. Her anxiety was winding up and about to scream like women do in the movies. I did not need that next to me.

"Nah," I said as I shook my head. "We have lots of altitude and another good engine that can get us back," I responded. Actually, I was not certain!

"Really?" her eyes pleaded. "Are you a pilot?"

"Nope, just a pastor," I replied.

"Oh, good," she began, "because God wouldn't kill you!" That sounded reassuring to me, as if the Lord used her voice to say, "I received your prayer!"

"You're right," I said, adding "God has a purpose in my life."

"I wish I could say the same," she lamented.

"Tell me about that," I said, hoping that this conversation could be a God-moment. It took her only a few minutes to off-load her life story... terrible childhood, two divorces from alcoholics, and four deadbeat children who lived off of her.

This was another Divine Appointment. I was exactly where I was supposed to be. When she was at the end of her story, I asked my usual question.

"What would you like the Lord to do for you?"

"I need peace in my life," she answered, "...in my family."

As we approached the airfield, we held hands and I prayed a simple blessing on her. It was a God-Moment.

"Thank you," she said, tears in her eyes, "I have waited a long time for this conversation."

We finally arrived at our chosen destination and Beth, the lady who picked me up, had also waited four hours for that one hour-flight. "We watched your flight on the radar on our laptops," she started. Most airlines have a flight tracer feature on their websites. "Did you know you disappeared off the radar?"

"We did?" I asked. When a plane disappears off the radar, it is a bad sign. Hearing her comment was unsettling and I asked, "What did you think had happened?"

"We figured you crashed. I prayed for your safety," she said.

Report 16   Death Notifications

A young volunteer approached me to ask if I could help an elderly man sitting in a wheelchair. She was anxious to return to him where four other youth volunteers were crouched around him. She jogged on ahead of me.

I could not keep up with this teenager and fell way behind her. By the time I arrived at the old gentleman's side, I was panting and completely out of breath. He sat quietly with a cane across his lap like a restraining bar on an old Ferris Wheel. Still wearing his Sunday suit, he was the picture of dignity.

Gasping for air, I tried to speak and finally blurted out, "Sorry... I'm out of breath... Grandfather... What is your name?" I always start with a simple fact question in order to help victims/survivors rein in their thoughts and more easily regain their orientation and sense of self. They are often in shock or pain and a simple fact question is appropriate.

"What is your name?" requires very little in the way of a response.

"Joseph," he answered, softly. With me kneeling down beside him, we were at eye level and I asked him a faith question.

"What would you like the Lord to do for you, Joseph?" I did not know any of his background or what he was currently experiencing. I continued to catch my breath and waited for him to speak.

I knew that my time with him was brief because others, like Joseph, were also waiting for some hope and a kind word. The extreme circumstances of this disaster forced me to skip all the other debrief questions that I would normally use as a Pastor to ease the person into a more comfortable emotional state.

"I would like to have the Lord care for my wife," he said in his gravelly, aged voice.

"What is your wife's name?" I asked him.

"Sheila," he replied, and added, "She's in a wheelchair."

"I would be glad to check on her condition," I assured him. I had no direct knowledge of her condition, but hopefully finding out about his wife Sheila would help ease his anxiety.

He then told me that she was "taken upstairs" after she felt pain in her chest, but he did not know where. I knew. The place he was describing had been dubbed the Black Tag Room which I had helped set up a day earlier.

It was the morgue. It was where the dead and near dead were placed. He had no idea what news was awaiting him.

The youth worker was joined by another and together, the three of us walked upstairs and down a very long hall to the

Black Tag Room. Each person in that room had been placed on a cot, except one elderly woman who sat in a wheelchair. It was Sheila.

She was slumped forward and looked like many of the folks I have seen in nursing homes. Straps across her chest restrained her from falling forward out of the chair, but she did not look asleep... she looked dead.

I am uncertain how it is that a person looks dead, but they do, even to an untrained eye like mine. It might be the absolute absence of life in the skin, the muscles, the very stillness of death. We approached her and I felt her hand strapped to the arm of the wheelchair.

I loathe touching dead flesh, but once again I had to. As usual, my senses were startled when I felt her skin, hard underneath the surface and cold to the touch. Like I just said, the absolute absence of life.

"She is already cold," I said to the youth workers.

I knelt down beside Sheila along with the youth workers. Huddled around her, I said, "Let's pray. Lord, thank you for the life of Sheila. We trust you to receive her into Your kingdom. Amen."

I remembered Joseph waiting for news about his wife and added, "Lord, help Joseph also. His life-long partner just died and this will be tough on him. Help Joseph deal with his own needs in all this chaos. Lord, please come near to him and let him sense your presence," I prayed earnestly.

When I speak to the Lord, there are no Thee's or Thou's, and none of the proper King James Version prayers by rote, just simple requests and thank-you's from the heart. Nothing for show; all for comfort and peace.

"Would you be willing," I asked the two youth workers, "to return with me to help do the death notification?" Both agreed even though they did not know what a death notification entailed. Still, I was impressed with their willingness to remain in the messiness of what needs to be done during a disaster.

We returned at a more leisurely pace and along the way I explained, "When doing a death notification, you basically say, 'I have terrible news, your wife has died.'"

I told them that this short, blunt sentence leaves no misunderstanding of the message. Euphemisms for death will only lead to confusion. It is easier for us, the messengers, to say, "She is gone," or "She has passed," when we actually mean, "She is dead and you will not see her alive ever again."

I told my two young volunteers, "Lengthy breaking of the news allows the listener to form false hope, so early on you have to use the word 'dead' or 'died'". When we give them mixed messages, we are not doing them a favor. The person giving the death notification must understand that relaying simple, direct, honest facts is always best.

People can handle the truth. They may react with crying or shock, but the truth can be understood even though the message is unwelcomed. I explained that the only reason I would give a circuitous explanation is to avoid the pain for me!

Trying to minimize their pain would be just my way of saying, "I do not want to be the one who brings the pain and I do not want their pain to hurt me," all of which is just plain selfishness on my part. I coached them on the Human Cry and the necessity of silently listening and being a peaceful presence.

Being on a disaster team involves many unpleasant duties; this is one of them. There is no way around it. It is my job, so I do it. When I see people's reactions to being told about a death, I experience part of their pain and often I tear up along with them.

Death hurts, but this is a part of what I am called to do as a Disaster Pastor. When we returned to Joseph, I knelt down slowly beside him, as if to pray.

"Joseph," I began, "I have terrible news. Your wife has died."

He flinched backward in his wheelchair, with surprise. I paused for a moment to let my words sink in and then asked, "Would you like to see your wife?"

"Of course," he said, seeming eager to do so.

"May a youth worker escort you to Shelia?" I asked.

He nodded in agreement. I looked up into the faces of the two young people to see if they were agreeable and they quickly expressed their willingness to escort Joseph. I backed away as the young man moved beside the grieving old man and began the sorrowful journey of guiding Joseph to his wife.

One of the many important services we offer as chaplains is referring people to resources they need. By handing Joseph over to the youth volunteers, in essence I referred him to people eager to help; people with time to spend getting him what he needed... with enthusiasm not yet dulled by the overwhelming numbers in this disaster.

I hoped the young people could practice their skills of listening for his Human Cry. If Joseph did not talk, then they could practice being a peaceful presence.

I immediately began to refocus on others, recognizing that by delegating Joseph to these youth, I could connect with those who as yet had no one helping them.

After working for days at a disaster, the cumulative effects on me can be damaging. Focusing full-time on others, I can lose sight of what I need.

Unfortunately, I am sleep deprived and yet too tired to sleep.

Report 17   Sleeping with The Dead

Desperate for a nap, the only quiet place I could find was the morgue I had set up earlier. Under a large roll-out bleacher in the commandeered basketball arena was perfect for a quiet, dark place to sleep.

I told my squad leader, Lynn Jones, where I would be in case I was needed. He squinted his eyes trying to figure how I could sleep with the dead. It sounded creepy to him.

"It is the only quiet place around here," I answered his unspoken question. He dismissed me with a wave of his hand. I grabbed an empty body bag and stretched it on the floor in the midst of several occupied ones.

I was so exhausted, beyond sensibility, that I did not give a second thought to the dead souls surrounding me whom I could no longer help. Even so, I began to pray a blessing on the dead but fell asleep before I said, "Amen".

Only 20 minutes later, a team member came looking for me. He was told I could be found in the morgue under the bleachers. He pulled open the tarp that covered the entrance and stepped into the dark morgue. It was so dark he could not find me among the body bags.

"Padre," he whispered. Was he afraid he would wake the dead? I was in deep rem sleep and did not respond. He called out again, this time louder, "PADRE". He figured I would be the only one who would answer. Still no response.

Not only was the room dark, but it was understandably quiet. Then he heard snoring from a distant body bags. He pulled out his flashlight and scanned the room in the direction of my bellowing sinuses.

Stepping carefully around the occupied body bags he eventually reached the foot of my bag. To wake me he tapped the bottom of my right boot with toe of his boot.

Instantly I sat up and saw the black silhouette of a man standing over me... calling my name. He must have caught me in the middle of a bad dream.

He appeared like the Angel of Death. In fright I screamed as I sat up. He reacted by screaming back at me.

Now, I was awake.

Later, well past midnight, the team moved to a new work site, an airport terminal. The Logistic team members cordoned off a sleeping area, a twenty by twenty foot area between two airport luggage carousels. Some team members choose the luggage conveyer belt to become their sleeping space.

If we did not like the idea of sleeping on the sloping hard rubber surface of the conveyer belt, we could choose to sleep on the disgusting, filthy, hard tile floor. I chose the flat floor.

We rolled out our sleeping bags and placed our "go bags" where our heads would lie; that marked our spot. I spread out my bag and flopped down on it. There was nothing between the hard floor and my weary body besides my thin sleeping bag. Crystal, an experienced paramedic, placed her sleeping bag next to mine. Steve parked his bag on my other side.

Since this was my first deployment with this team, I wondered where we were supposed to change our clothes. It did not take long to learn. Crystal stood at the foot of her bag and began to disrobe. She had turned her back to me and shrugged off her khaki pants.

Yikes!

I averted my eyes.

I looked around and saw other team members unabashedly shedding their filthy work clothes for some semblance of night wear. I decided to swallow my embarrassment and try to look as normal as the rest of them, pretending by my behavior, "Sure, I do this all the time. This doesn't bother me."

I turned my back to the team and counted on the darkness to provide enough cover. I casually unbuckled my belt, letting my trousers drop to the floor. As my cargo pants fell, I realized my boots were still on both feet. I wished I had had the foresight to take them off first and reduce the exposure time.

I performed the subconscious ritual of holding the back of one shoe down with the toe of the other foot. After that exercise in slow motion, I finally removed my clergy shirt.

I stood in the darkness, wishing desperately that I was a boxer shorts guy – they sort of look like tennis shorts and feel a little less revealing. Wearing a tee shirt and my tighty-whities, I quickly crawled into my bag where sleep overcame the hardness of the floor and all my inhibitions.

After years with the team, all those inhibitions have surprisingly vanished. Despite the clamor in the airport, the thirty-six of us slept undisturbed, peacefully, like the dead nearby.

The following night, an unknown generous source provided us with cots. Each of us grabbed one like drowning people lurching for a life raft. Getting elevated off the contaminated floor felt like a medical necessity, not just a luxury. The cots came ten to a box and the box was about the size of a washing machine.

I grabbed one of the empty cartons and placed it at the head of my sleep area, then tucked the top portion of my cot inside the box. It only went halfway in, but when I was lying on the cot, my head was inside it.

The box became my cave and my respite. It blocked out all the lights and muffled the stirring of people, giving me a little sanctuary. After the chaos of the day's events, the box helped my soul relax from the peoples' cries around us.

I felt like I had private luxury accommodations. Of course, my concept of "luxury" had been redefined to mirror the austere circumstances.

Tucked into my cardboard box, I could not see the chaos outside, but my brain turned into a 3-D IMAX theater screen. For hours I replayed the catastrophes of the day until exhaustion overcame me and I fell asleep.

Report 18   The Expectant Room

I had set up another morgue at a new site. A few days earlier, it was a large room where 180 passengers assembled to board their departing plane. Satisfied that the room was ready to receive the dead, I left for work with the living.

The next day, I returned to the morgue only to find it had become an Expectant Room. In disaster language, an Expectant Room is not for birthing mothers like you would assume, but is a room to house those victims who were not expected to survive.

Initially, the idea was repulsive and reprehensible to me. How could we relegate the near dead to their own waiting room... and let them die? I assumed that if a person were placed in the Expectant Room, they would remain there until death.

Later, I would learn that patients do get reassessed and could be moved out as resources became available. However, that first time, I did not know this and was horrified that the still-living were among those who were already dead.

Upon entering, I saw that there were two long rows of patients lying on cots low to the floor. In a quick scan of the room, I could see that most of the people were alive. My practice as a Chaplain was to kneel beside each bed and briefly visit with the person. If they were able to reply, I would ask their name and what had happened to them.

After a few minutes, I prayed a blessing on them and moved to the next person. I worked my way about halfway down the row, kneeling down and praying for each.

Then as I knelt beside an older woman suddenly she reached out and grabbed my hand. She could not talk, but she gripped my hand so tightly that she was crushing my knuckles.

No man has ever squeezed my hand so hard. Instinctively, this felt like a death grip – odd that in my chosen line of work, I had not encountered this before. Her blue eyes looked into my eyes and she pulled my face within three inches of her face.

We were much too close for comfort. I tried to pull away, but she had superhuman strength that pulled me right back.

She could not talk and I assumed that she was a stroke victim. But, her desperate eyes were alert and clearly communicated, "I know where I am. If you don't get me out of here, they will let me die!"

After what seemed like long minutes of staring into one another's eyes, I managed to pry her fingers off my wrist and free myself. I walked over to the charge nurse standing behind a ticket counter.

"Why are these people here?" I asked indignantly. "This is supposed to be a morgue."

"This is the Expectant Room," she began, "and they have been placed here by the Chief Medical Officer because they are expected to die." I took a step back, surprised by her answer.

Several thoughts and emotions jammed my brain. I was appalled, horrified and confused. I glanced around quickly to see if anyone on nearby cots had heard her comment.

"But, you have seen me talking with several of these people," I shot back. All they need is some water and minimal care!" I explained.

"Well, that's the way it is," she said. She was stretched beyond her breaking point and had kicked into zombie mode – she was just following orders and no longer connecting with the dire circumstances.

I could not imagine that anyone in normal life would say, "it's just the way things are." I would like to think that she was on empty and not really able to undo the unnecessary death sentence imposed upon these people.

If one of my family members were in this place, I hope somebody would step up and help. How could anyone look at these folks and not agree that some of them could survive? Not all of them, granted, but why not the ones we could save?

Several of the older ladies reminded me of my grandmother and a few of the men had eyes like my father. Somebody had to step up and help.

"I am going to find another Chief Medical Officer. Some of these people don't belong here," I protested. Once again, righteous anger overwhelmed my blinding fatigue.

Storming down the concourse, I found another doctor, one from my medical team. After explaining the situation, I begged, umm, directed him, "Go down there and see if there are any you can get out of the morgue!"

Several hours later, that same charge nurse found me and reported that the doctor I'd sent got four people out of the Expectant Room. I should have been ecstatic. Instead, I felt deeply frustrated because I knew there were others who were very much alive when I left.

I never found out if the vise grip grandma were among the four. After all, she had put her hope in me that I would do something. The next day, the Expectant Room was empty.

One of my tasks is to give people hope. What happens to people who give up hope?

Report 19   The Power of No Hope

On one mission of mercy, we had set up our medical station to triage people in a large shelter - women giving birth, those who had been raped, bludgeoned and shot, along with other medical emergencies.

I felt excited at the prospect of going into the heart of pandemonium. It hardly fits my image as a seasoned pastor, but under my thin veneer of maturity is still that young boy who is thrilled to be where the action is, the place where I can be of the most help.

I approached the doors of this huge building turned-shelter that warehoused disaster victims. It was far from ideal, but it was all that was available to accommodate the thousands of folks who had not been able to evacuate in time.

Busloads of victims, survivors and evacuees arrived one after another. Every effort was made to establish some sort of order and normalcy.

The overwhelming numbers made it chaotic to house that many people in a confined space. The place was large enough; that was not the issue. The issue was that there was not

enough of anything to make it habitable, much less comfortable
and accommodating.

There was no water, sanitary facilities, food or sleeping
quarters, and no way for families to create boundaries to
designate their parcel of concrete.

Think about it, when sporting events are held in similar
large facilities and thousands of people are jammed into a
limited space, people do not wander all over the playing field . .
. they are sitting in the stands cheering their team. The
spectators are mostly well-behaved, some are rowdy and a little
drunk, but for the most part, it is a manageable crowd out for a
good time.

People tacitly accept that there will always be more than
enough to meet their needs and whims, that there would
always be more of everything available. If you want something,
you just have to pay for it.

Just tell one of the hundreds of volunteers in their branded
vests and ID badges that the toilet paper is running low and they
immediately take care of it.

None of this was an option in the horrible days after the
disaster. All the usual amenities were either absent or
overwhelmed.

At first, everyone was so thankful to be alive and have dry
land under their feet. But that quickly changed. The lack of

needed supplies caused not just inconvenience, but along with the heat made the conditions inside unbearable.

At this disaster, I was able to go inside the shelter to get an up close view of what we as a medical team might be dealing with. For starters, outdoors was hot and humid. Inside, it was worse: no electricity, no air conditioning, no security, no food, no water or ice. No toilet paper.

Perspiration rose like smog over the miserable people languishing in the dark space. The suffering was only magnified by the $100°$ temperature and 99% humidity.

Inside, babies were without hope of clean diapers and wore their soiled ones until they were so loaded up that they were discarded into the overflowing trash receptacles.

Restrooms were designed for random visits during 3-hour sports events, but now the toilets were overwhelmed and failed. They overflowed into the rest of the building and it became fecal swamps, with the slippery floors carrying all kinds of diseases.

It was dreadful. There was nothing any of us could do.

As I squeezed through the narrow opening into the shelter, one of the guards flippantly remarked, "Good luck!" Why was he wishing me luck? A memory from my childhood flashed across my mind. I was getting on a carnival ride, The Chamber of Horrors, for the first time. Above the entrance, the sign read: "Abandon All Hope. All Are Doomed."

At the time, I had nervously asked the ride operator about an empty car coming through the exit door and he replied with malice, "Oh, those people didn't make it." He was shaking his head as he fastened the safety bar across my lap and said with a sneer, "Good luck!"

Even with my eyes wide open and adjusting to the dimly lit shelter, I could not at first understand what I saw. My physical senses could not assimilate everything that was going on around me. I felt confused, disoriented.

A horrible sense of dread washed over me, as if a gloomy unnatural presence, a dark malevolent and very evil spirit, loomed over the crowd, creating a great sense of oppression against them.

People saw my clergy collar and gave way as another team member and I waded into the dense crowd. Those first few moments in the disaster shelter stimulated the same terror that the carnival ride had conjured up in my young mind.

This shelter felt frightening, alarming. I wondered if those inside had succeeded in their heroic escapes from the floodwaters only to succumb to this black hole of despair and squalor.

My first thought was that these people were Americans on American soil. They should never ever be treated this way. Humane services to those inside had dissolved with the failed air conditioning, as well as the absence of toilet facilities, food and water.

Plus, there was no way for anyone to leave this shelter. The task of the guards at the doors was to keep people in and not allow them to leave. However, inside the shelter nobody protected them from the worst of human nature.

Dangerous gang members, rapists - all who had entered the shelter came with their best and worst. In my mind, I was shouting, "Somebody with authority, DO SOMETHING!" In these wretched conditions, I saw nothing done to make life safe and livable.

I was moving among the people, talking with them, offering prayers and trying to encourage them. These people had lost everything except their lives. "Even though I walk through the valley of the shadow of death," I prayed over the people and reassured myself, "I will fear no evil, for you are with me."[9]

A few minutes earlier, people were passive for the most part. They appeared orderly and clustered with family or

---

[9] Twenty-third Psalm

friends. Some clung to each other, which is an important survival instinct; it is harder to attack two than one.

By being close to someone else, there is a measure of safety, even if only in the mind. We feel less vulnerable to maliciousness or physical harm.

In an instant, the mood changed and the appearance of my clergy collar triggered shouting and rushing waves of people. Hands reached out from nowhere and pulled at me, beseeching me for blessings, prayers, help of all kinds.

I could feel myself being pulled under by the clutching hands of genuinely desperate people, fellow Americans. Overtaken by their numbers and astonished at their needs, I drew back as they lurched at me with a frightening urgency.

They meant me no harm. Maybe they thought I had come with food and water, but it was just me. I brought nothing, no food, no answers to their prayers, no solutions to relieve their suffering.

I felt fear rising in me, not of the people themselves, but of the enormity of the disaster and the lack of resources available.

What did I think I was doing, strolling into a roiling caldron of needy, desperate people who just wanted what we all want: water, food, shelter and dignity.

However, I was helpless and they were hopeless.

These were not bad people; they were legitimately in despair and their circumstances were dire and life-threatening.

Some had not had time to grab life-saving medications; others became separated from their families with no means of learning their fates; all of them were severely traumatized by the flood and by an uncaring bureaucracy.

Young men scrambled over older folks sitting in folded seats, wild eyes turned to me; and children waved their arms to get my attention. Scores of scattered groups turned into waves of the incautious, making an ever-tightening circle around me.

I soon became enveloped by those crammed in the shelter; their urgency became a compelling force. Their overwhelming needs were past critical and they were creating a dangerous situation for me.

Many of these folks probably attended a local church before the disaster hit. Today, this same group, through no fault of their own, was forming into a spontaneous and determined mob. They were losing hope of ever getting four things: water, food, cleanliness and freedom.

A few minutes earlier, I did not fear these people. Now, there was panic in their eyes. Knowing that panic could flash over into mob action landed on me like hot grease, fast and painful. I had to get out.

My chances for making a safe exit were rapidly diminishing. I could hear the stereo "Good luck!" from the guard outside the shelter and the long-ago carnival ride operator. Escaping would require more than luck.

"Lord, get me out of here," I prayed. I turned around and retreated from that dark chamber towards the light I knew was outside the shelter. By now, hundreds more people jammed the portal I had entered such a short time ago.

My shoulders turned left and then right to cut through tiny spaces between tightly-packed bodies. Reaching those exterior doors would be the longest one hundred feet I had ever traveled, if I made it. That may sound like soap opera drama, but it accurately describes my dire situation and fear level.

Hands reached out from everywhere, grabbing at every piece of fabric I wore and at my hands, arms and legs, pulling hard in every direction. I knew these grips were from people locked into truly horrible conditions and now, I too could also feel a special touch of misery and hopelessness.

Slowly, I forced my way through the packed bodies as I heard snippets of conversation and begging voices.

"Can you get me out of here?"

"Help! Please help us!"

"My baby needs milk!"

They were vulnerable and someone needed to help them. At that moment I could not save myself. I too felt trapped, abandoned and alone. Panic began to rise inside of me.

Their faces pressed against mine. Their desperate, innocent eyes pleaded to get out. Yet their eyes asked for something more:

"Can you give me hope?"

As the saying goes, eyes are the windows to the soul, the inner life. These people had lost hope. Those desperate eyes still haunt me. I can still see them now, anytime, anywhere.

Why were they without hope? Not just because they had no food or water for days. They had lost hope for one primal reason: they had no prospect of freedom. They felt the guards were not acting as their protectors, but as bullies to keep them physically captive.

Those trapped had been told by authorities, "I will try to get you out of here." That became a broken promise. I knew better than to repeat it. My goal was to escape with my life. My survival instinct switched on.

"I *WILL* get you out of here!" I shouted boldly, but falsely. Looking back, I should have said nothing than to lie. In the moment, however, I feared that saying nothing or uttering the word "try" would ensure my inadvertent demise.

Suddenly their hands relaxed and stopped tearing at me. It felt like a miracle had just happened for me. Did God use my lie?

I stepped through their loosening grip, out of the darkness, into the 100^0 Southern sunlight. Even the 99% humidity felt like a fresh ocean breeze hitting my face. The hot sun seemed to burn away the oppressive dimness from my soul. I felt hope pushing aside the darkness within me.

"I am free," I prayed, "but all those people are still suffering inside, Lord," I said, shaking my head, "Please, have mercy and get them out." I begged forgiveness for my lie. "Lord, forgive me, please."

Since that narrow escape, I have studied riots and revolutions. I am convinced of these two facts: Riots do not begin when people overcome their fear... if they feel fear, they still have something to lose. Rather, riots and revolutions begin when people lose their hope. Truly, people without hope have nothing to lose.

A hopeless man is far more dangerous than a fearless one.

Lesson Learned: After four days of no food, water or hope, the Beast comes out in all of us.

Report 20   The Power of Symbol

During a disaster, survivors will often identify a tangible symbol of hope. We have a primal need, a Human Cry, to dedicate time, a space or an object as a memorial or monument of an important, life-changing event.

At a disaster, as I move from person to person, I will occasionally see a hand clutching an object suspended on chains around their necks, particularly the women. I had only to ask the first one I encountered what she had in her hand and she opened it to show me a tiny Cross. That explained all of the other poor souls with hands holding tightly to their only tangible symbol of their genuine hope, in her case, Jesus Christ.

"Why are you holding onto the Cross?" I asked.

"I have nothing," the woman said, "but I can hold onto this Cross and that gives me peace."

Walking among the waves of people, I reflected on her simple statement. The Cross, whether a Crucifix with Jesus hanging on it or an empty Cross symbolizing Jesus' resurrection from the dead, has been a symbol of suffering, of hope of forgiveness from sin and an expectation of eternal life. And in a disaster, the Cross gives people something solid to hold onto while chaos swirls around them.

Why should a two-thousand year old instrument of execution that inflicted such pain and suffering, give modern day people in disasters hope?

Another symbol seen in the aftermath of the attacks on the Twin Towers, the Pentagon, and in the Pennsylvania field, was the American flag. Many who witnessed the events of 9/11, whether firsthand or on TV, were caught up in an immense surge of patriotism.

American flags hung from freeway overpasses, streamed behind pickup trucks and from front porches. It felt good to be united. Perhaps our focus on the American flag was an in-your-face challenge to al Qaeda.

Or, perhaps it was our attempt at trying to shove our disbelief and shock into the background and refocus on what was excellent in America.

A remarkable number of people went back to church. Some wanted a renewed closeness to God, but others longed to make more sense of the tragedy and acts of evil.

Each evening as I returned to Ground Zero, the landscape invariably changed as the cranes and earthmovers sliced and chewed their way through the rubble. Buildings disappeared as the crews cleared them away and the mammoth machines would create new landmarks, different landscapes and new orientations each day and night.

With so many visual changes and no durable focal points, I regularly lost my sense of direction. My inner compass just spun around.

I had gotten acquainted with a NYC police officer, Rich, at one of the checkpoints which I had to clear each time I descended into The Pit. One particular night, a special, holy night, would become my personal God-moment at Ground Zero.

Rich and I stood facing the Pile as a thousand workers moved around like well-organized ants, driven toward the common goal of removing debris and searching for any remnants of nearly 2,000 souls who had not been accounted for.

"Rich," I complained, "every time I come here, the place changes. I get disoriented. Do you ever get disoriented?"

"Nope, not anymore," Rich answered with certainty.

"Why not?" I asked. Then, with his arm stretched out and his index finger extended, he pointed to an area at least a hundred yards away, to the other side of the debris field.

"Do you see that Cross over there?" he asked.

He pointed to a unique and perfectly formed Cross, discovered by a crane operator just two days after the Towers

fell. The crane operator was Frank Silecchia, one of the biggest
humans I have ever seen, with a deceptively gentle spirit!

Frank Silecchi and the WTC Cross, © groundzeromuseumworkshop.com

When I spoke to Frank, he said that he had seen something
familiar at the bottom of The Pile and gingerly picked his way
with his crane to verify that what he thought he saw was real –
it took his breath away. It was a Cross; he had not imagined it.

Amidst the twisted steel, rebar and concrete, he was
amazed to be looking at two I-beams, shaped into a perfect
Cross 20 feet high and 4,000 pounds of the now re-purposed,
hardened steel. Those around him looked reverently, in
disbelief, at the same sight.

On top of one of the horizontal crossbeams was a piece of sheet metal that looked as if it had been carefully arranged to suggest a shroud. Many wept, some dropped to their knees.

Steel workers clambered down to the bottom of The Pit as fast as they could move, disregarding all the hazards that could have easily inflicted injuries. They seemed to feel a great sense of urgency. With torches, they cut off the bottom and lifted it by crane, placing it on a pedestal at the entrance to the World Trade Center Park.

All who entered Ground Zero would now walk past this precious symbol, standing silently for all to see, knowing it had emerged from beneath a mountain of rubble. It was not pristine; it was rugged. And it instantly became celebrated as a reassurance that there was hope: for the survivors, for all the Ground Zero workers and indeed, for a grieving nation.

"Terrorism brought the buildings down," Officer Rich said, "but the Cross built up our faith." He surmised that when the building collapsed, it sheared off the sides and the top, shaping a perfect Cross.

"When you find the Cross," he continued, "you always know where you are." I believe Rich meant that the Cross was a visible landmark to help establish one's bearings.

Then came my own God-moment.

That Cross, both symbolic and tangible, remained unseen at the bottom of the Pile, waiting in the dark to make a proclamation that where there is evil, grace abounds. It does not matter how deep The Pit or how wide The Pile, the Cross would be found under it.

That ancient symbol of suffering brought hope to a thousand workers gathered at the rim of The Pit as each one stood silently, pondering its meaning. God was reminding us that humans have free will to do evil or good, and that God will seldom interfere with that free will. However, in the midst of unthinkable darkness, we can cling to the Cross.

After all these decades, I still do not fully understand the Cross or its unwavering power to transform lives. However, in my life I have observed this singularity:

After death comes life. After crucifixion comes resurrection.

I do not know why, but it always works in that order. When people find themselves buried under their own piles of rubble, I point them to the Cross.

After the Cross emerged, I asked hundreds of workers what seeing the Cross meant to them. Their message was profound:

When evil takes its best shot at us

and it did;

When we suffer loss because of evil,

and we do;

When we ask the question WHY,

and we have;

We will find the Cross at the bottom of the rubble.

The Cross stands silently, and proclaims a bold message.

The Cross overcomes evil with acts of faith, hope and love.

Report 21   The 90 Second Rule

In preparation for sending a group of physicians and nurses on a medical mission, I was assigned to brief them on ethical decisions they would face. My job was to preemptively counsel them, to prepare them in hopes of lessening the shock that comes with such decisions.

We were already at the staging site, but these physicians and nurses had not yet been exposed to the terrible reality that awaited them. They listened with visible disbelief, especially when I discussed the 90-second rule.

This 90-second rule is used when a surge of patients thoroughly overwhelms the medical waiting area and there is not sufficient time to thoroughly assess and adequately treat each one; hence the limitation of 90 seconds per patient. All treatment, from first glance to their exit, cannot last longer than 90 seconds. If the medical personnel took longer, then the patient load stacked up exponentially.

It should be noted that no one stands over the patient with a stopwatch and tosses them out of their chair when the time is up. However, disaster medical personnel use a fast paced method they call *treat and street*. Our specific goal is to stabilize and transport patients to a place where medical care can be more thorough.

Standing in front of me were 35 experienced ER specialists and medical champions who had never deployed before. The medical team I was briefing was fresh from their efficient offices and high tech hospitals. The day before they were accustomed to having adequate time to diagnose patients with ample access to additional specialists, tests and supplies.

Out here the conditions were austere. Triaging hundreds of people out in the hot sun and humidity would require a different medical model. Tending to the injured in a rubble field required them to learn a whole new skill set.

Instead of using electricity for their high-tech instruments, they would rely on high-touch skills. Instead of sterile conditions, they would most likely do amputations on a dirt trail with swarms of flies landing on the wound. Instead of using antibiotics to prevent infection, they would transport them onto someone else and silently wish their patients good luck.

Instead of measuring their success by the best possible outcome for the patient, they would have to determine what's best for the community. They would have to manage their guilt, knowing that if only they had the tools back home, these people would have a good chance of living.

Given these austere conditions, they would be forced to suspend their high standards of care and lengthy workups that lead to accurate diagnoses and then excellent medical intervention.

"You will find yourselves making decisions," I told them, "that you know only God should be allowed to make." After giving this briefing, I must have sounded very matter of fact, perhaps cavalier. One doctor standing at the back, behind other medical personnel, challenged my ethical model.

"I have been an ER doc for twenty-five years," he began. "I have seen it all and done it all. What you are saying is not true."

"I have done numerous disasters since 9/11," I wanted to reply, "I know for a fact what is going to happen to you." However, I said nothing. I felt humiliated that he had so confidently dismissed my briefing in front of all his colleagues; rejecting the help I was trying to impart. After all, he was an expert ER doctor and I was just a Disaster Pastor in their collective eyes.

Then, to add more humiliation, he added a zinger: "Why don't you stick to the preaching and leave the medicine to us?" There were chuckles and harrumphs of agreement. Ouch! His words stung. Part of me wanted to respond in kind, but I held my tongue and kept a pleasant expression on my face.

"When you return from your first Strike Team, come talk to me afterward," I responded. The only comfort I had was in knowing that he would soon discover that what I had taught was true. "I would love to hear about what you experienced."

He agreed. I walked away like a dog with its tail between its legs. It took a while to shake off the embarrassment of my sincere efforts to forewarn them of what they should expect. If only they could have taken seriously what I was telling them.

Twelve hours later, the same confident ER doc returned from his first mission. He was looking for me. Inwardly I groaned, not knowing what to expect, but anticipating more demeaning sound bites.

"Oh, I'm so glad I found you," he started out. "You were wrong about the 90 seconds."

"Here we go," I thought. I planted my feet apart, keeping my arms loose, doing my best to look approachable and friendly. Standing behind him was his entire delegation from the morning's session. I instantly assumed they joined the doctor to compound my embarrassment!

"Okay, I am really interested to hear what happened out there," I said. Actually, I wanted to avoid another confrontation, but I am a nice guy and had a mother who taught me to be polite.

"It was more like 50 seconds, not 90," he announced.

I was startled by his admission. I had not seen this one coming.

"The nurse and I triaged over eight hundred people, about one hundred an hour – ALL DAY!" He was eager to tell me his story.

"I had about two hundred patients left and only an hour before we had to leave the area." It was imperative that they catch the armed escort ride back to camp at the departure time or they would be stuck there all night without protection.

"Wow! What did you do?" I asked.

"I grabbed a magic marker and walked through the throngs of waiting patients."

"A magic marker?"

"Based on a glance," he paused, overcome with emotion, "I put a plus or minus mark on each person's forehead." He was so choked up, he spoke more slowly, like a judge rendering his decision "I made the minus mark and people were moved over to a shady spot away from our medical area.

"The ones with a plus mark stayed seated on the ground and got their 50 seconds of medical attention." He hung his head, as if he were the one being judged.

"And what about the God part?" I asked gently.

"I became..." he paused while shaking his bowed head back and forth, "God. It wasn't right that I decided who lived and who died." He got it. I taught that point to his team earlier that morning. A disaster team makes life and death decisions when deciding "treat now or treat later."

"I am so sorry you had to go through that," I said. There was no pleasure in being exonerated or validated. I just felt sadness that he now understood the merciless realities of disaster medical work. In a mass casualty disaster, triage can seem as cruel, but in reality, it is the best method that ensures so many can be saved.

"What was your reaction to what you did today?" I asked.

"I loathe myself," he said and began sobbing. Several of his colleagues standing around him drew closer, putting their hands on his shoulders to comfort him.

"We needed you to do exactly what you did," I assured him, speaking loudly enough for the whole group to hear. "The Lord is pleased that you helped so many people. You did the right thing."

Hours earlier he rejected my message; now he understood. The next day, I asked the same doctor how he knew to place a plus or minus on someone's forehead.

"Is this person salvageable?" he answered. This is the irreducible essence of the triage model. Especially in austere conditions, it makes sense to do the most good for the most people rather than concentrating personnel and limited resources on the worst cases first.

Triage works best when the responders are emotionally detached from the victims. Triaging would be messy if the responders know or are related to the victims.

However, if my grandchild were buried in rubble, the triage model would strike me as barbaric, irrelevant, immoral and unethical. Dismissing the needs of everyone else, I would move heaven and earth to rescue my little boy or girl, my grandson or granddaughter. Nothing would stop me.

Report 22   Repo Man

I jumped on a plane wearing my clergy collar to attend the Presidential Prayer Breakfast that met the following day. Specifically, my role would be to pray with dignitaries from the US and around the world as they came to the Prayer Room.

We squeezed into seats in the cheap peasant section of a major airlines flight. After everyone was settled in, the cabin doors shut. A flight attendant ordered, "Cross check". One of these days I will find out what that actually means.

Then, a tired looking flight attendant directed our attention to the TV monitors that dropped down from the ceiling. This was the safety video that reminded us "that in the unlikely event that we loose cabin pressure, place the oxygen mask on yourself first then place it on your child."

We were 30 seconds into this safety video when we heard a loud banging on the fuselage. A man was standing at the end of the jet way ramp pounding his fist on the outside of our plane. His persistent and forceful knocks demanded entrance.

I assumed he was a very late passenger who felt entitled and very determined to catch this flight. Flight attendants near the main cabin door looked at each other wondering what to do.

"Flight attendants, please open the door," ordered the Captain over the loud speaker.

A man in his 30s dressed in a blue suit stepped through the opened door and past the three flight attendants. They did not know what to make of this strange visitor. Without smiling or greeting them, he took an immediate left and walked directly up to the secured door to the flight deck. The man held papers in his left hand and with his right hand pounded loudly on the Captain's door. The door opened. The man entered the small space behind the pilot's seats and the door closed behind him.

A minute passed. None of us were watching the video that was showing us how to use our seat cushions as floatation devises in case we make a water landing. Besides, there is not much water between Los Angeles and Washington DC.

"This is the Captain," he began. "In my 20 years of flying, I have never had this happen." What? The Captain's voice that usually sounds like the voice of God now sounded confused, befuddled. "This is a first for me." The man who demanded entrance onto the plane served legal papers on the pilot.

"Wells Fargo has just repossessed our plane!" Huh? You mean the airlines did not pay their bill to Wells Fargo? Apparently not. The Captain ordered us off the plane and promised to put us on another flight.

All 195 souls on board gathered their belongings and assembled in the same terminal gate area where we had earlier waited to get on this now empty plane.

A pilot walked up and stood next to me in the terminal.

With his hand clutching the pull handle of his luggage he seemed to be wondering what to do next like the rest of us. I did not know if he were the same pilot who gave us the message to get off the plane or just hitching a ride.

"What is your reaction to what happened?" I asked him. This is an open-ended question that is a standard conversation starter for me. Men always have reactions and I figured he had several.

"He was a repo man," he stated as he more clearly realized what had just happened.

Another pilot walked up beside me. "Getting bumped from this plane is how the rest of my life is going," he complained.

"How so?" I asked.

"Oh, you don't have the time," he said as if testing me to see if I would really take the time to hear his story.

"Tell me what is happening. I'm interested." We stood at the large window overlooking our repossessed jumbo jet.

Noticing my clergy collar, he began, "Okay, I just learned my wife is having an affair." He paused, seeing if I wanted to listen to more.

"I'm so sorry. You must feel terribly betrayed," I said with empathy. "Tell me more."

"My teenage son is on drugs and my daughter hates me for some reason." I was standing next to a Divine Appointment, a conversation planned and lead by God. This man needed someone to hear his story.

We gazed aimlessly out the window when our attention was drawn to a tug as it drove around the building and parked in front of the 757. The driver stepped off the tug and hitched a tow bar to the front landing gear of the giant plane. He climbed back onto his seat and waited for three other ground crew members to take their positions around the plane.

One stood below the left and right wing tips and the third placed himself at the rear of the plane. Because the tug operator was about to push the plane into a traffic lane where other planes were coming and going, it was the task of the three ground crew member lookouts to make sure that their plane was not pushed into another plane.

Once the three-member lookout crew was in position, the tug revved up its big engine and a black plume of exhaust belched from its tail pipe. With brute force, the tug slowly pushed the 220,000-pound airplane away from the gate.

"This must be a very hard time for you," I said, continuing my conversation with the gentleman next to me. "I know that God loves you and is able to help."

"Yeah, I used to be a Christian, but I just drifted away," he explained.

"Can I pray a blessing on you?" I have asked this question thousands of times to people in every possible walk of life. Not once has anyone declined my offer. They have all wanted a blessing. Everyone, atheists, followers of other gods and even the non-religious have been open to receiving a blessing.

"Here?" He looked around to see if anyone were watching. "Now?" He may have been afraid I would embarrass him by putting on a freak show with frenzied prayer.

"Yes," I answered. Not knowing what I might do, he summoned his courage. What he did not know was that I never embarrass someone when they are vulnerable.

"Lord," I began in a normal conversational voice, "You love this precious man." We continued to look out the window and appeared like everyone else who was having a regular conversation. "Draw him back to yourself. Be with him as he loves and helps his family. Amen."

"That's it?" he said, perhaps relieved that nothing strange had happened. "Well, what I really should say is, 'Thank you.'" He turned to me and tears began to run down his face. "I have hardened my heart to my family and I need to love them. That is what they want from me."

"The Lord will be with you and help you," I said. He nodded his head in agreement. "Get reconnected with the Lord and trust that the rest will work out." Our Divine Appointment was over.

"The Lord is with you," I reminded him. But, I was not expecting his response.

"And also with you," he answered.

God can use anything and anyone for a Divine Appointment, even a repo man.

Report 23   Fierce Courage

I was awakened in the middle of the night by my cell phone ringing. One of the disaster teams I serve asked me to deploy immediately.

There had been a devastating earthquake that ravaged an area known for its beauty and poverty. I had no inkling of the enormity of this massive earthquake and its awesome destructive power.

The quick facts: a million people were left homeless; more than a hundred thousand were dead. Almost a quarter of a million structures were flattened. Scores of people of all ages and status were still trapped between the layers of rubble.

When I arrived, I checked in with Colonel Michael Foster, who was in charge of the troops guarding us. He and his soldiers had been at the site for days before we arrived, so he had the knowledge we needed.

Col. Mike Foster and his wife, Reggie

A little background on Colonel Foster: He would eventually spend over 62 months in combat deployed to Iraq and Afghanistan. Not one to sit in the back, he regularly led patrols. He is one of the few who stepped on a landmine and survived. One night I observed a remarkable habit worth mentioning. When his soldiers lined up at the chow line for meals, he was the last one in a line of 400 Army Rangers. Same thing with the showers, when they were available, he was always last.

Soon after our team was on site, I met with Colonel Foster and asked, "What can we do to help?"

"Go to the camp and organize the eleven thousand families," he instructed. In my ignorance of what this monumental request would entail, I readily agreed.

I immediately joined a Strike Team to walk through the camp. Four armed soldiers escorted two medics, a communications' operator and me, the Chaplain. My assignment was to survey and assess the people's living conditions.

They could only be described as appalling. At this particular site, fifty thousand homeless, suffering people needed the basics: clean water, food, sanitation and somewhere safe to sleep.

As a community organizer and a student of the human condition, I instinctively knew what was necessary. I would need help and a lot of it. The first step was to connect with qualified and well-recognized leaders to accomplish the task.

Meandering through the mass of displaced humanity, I met two local pastors. They recognized me because I wore a clergy collar. After a brief conversation, I asked them to recruit as many local pastors as they could and join me the following morning at the Command Post at 9:00 a.m.

A Strike Team enters the camp

After several hours surveying the camp, our Strike Team eventually returned to the Command Post. I was physically exhausted and emotionally overwhelmed. I grabbed two bottles of water and slumped into the only empty chair under a cabana type shelter.

I took off my booney hat and poured the first bottle of water over my head, face and chest. I guzzled the second one, sensing that I was dangerously close to dehydration.

A few feet away sat a middle age man watching me try to cool down. He was obviously a new arrival because he was dressed in clean savanna type clothes. A reporter, a dignitary, a doctor? Although I was too spent for social conversation, our eyes connected and I felt obligated to introduce myself.

"Hi, I'm Padre."   He introduced himself as Dr. Michael Finegan, a psychologist from Boston. Dr. Finegan was a long ways from home and I wondered what brought him here. He reached into his cargo pants, pulled out an energy bar and handed it to me.

"Here, you look like you can use this," he said. I took it and ate it quickly. "I was sent by Mother Teresa's group, Sisters of Charity, as well by Donal Reily of Catholic Relief Services."   Both organizations are heavyweight players when it comes to disasters. My exhaustion disappeared. I sat up straight. This was a Divine Appointment.

I told Dr. Finegan about my task and that I had invited local pastors to join me the following morning at this very spot. Would he be available to meet with us?

The next morning, twelve pastors arrived at our command post in their finest suits. I handed each a bottle of water and invited them to huddle around a small table.

The appearance of this group reminded me of another group. We arrived "on the third day" and now we were sitting around a table with twelve holy men who would help resurrect the broken spirits of their countrymen... just as Jesus sat with his twelve disciples around a table before his crucifixion and resurrection.

Dr. Michael Finegan

"I know you are grieving and broken-hearted, just like
everyone else in the camp," Dr. Finegan began. "But right now,
your people need you to lead them." Each one of these pastors
came to the meeting with deep sorrow and had a desperate
need to grieve his own loss. Eventually each of them would
grieve but not right now. He did not discourage them from
grieving, but "do not let your grieving stop you from leading."

"Later there will be time for tears, but not yet," he
challenged. I can still see their faces and feel their distress at
what we were asking of them. Each of these pastors had lost at
least one family member, the same as nearly all the rest of the
survivors.

Then, like an evangelist issuing an altar call, Dr. Finegan
asked for their commitment to lead the people with fierce
courage. He explained what he meant. He did not mean for

them to show angry or cruel courage, but "to be single-minded, determined and hopeful, even while you are heavy-laden with the deepest sadness."

Col. Foster explained fierce courage differently; he called it Midnight Courage. "The rarest form of courage is midnight courage. Not courage displayed against known risks in the light of knowledge, but courage against the unknown... against unseen risks and dangers... that wait in the dark. It is courage in the form of events that occur in the darkest of nights and the darkest of times." Col. Foster knew fear and Midnight Courage. He led Army Ranger combat patrols for 53 months in Iraq and Afghanistan.

As Dr. Michael Finegan and I looked at these pastors, we knew the people would naturally follow these well-known and trusted community leaders. These pastors were making a sacrificial commitment to demonstrate fierce courage.

While they contained their own suffering, we needed them to be leaders/shepherds of their waiting flocks. We were looking for pastors who demonstrated these essential qualities of leadership.

At that point, our immediate task was to discern which one of these pastors could best lead the other pastors. We asked each of them to speak for about two minutes and give us his name, his church's name and a description of what his church might be able to bring to the effort, such as school rooms, medical facilities or playgrounds.

What Dr. Finegan and I also were listening for was a very humble pastor who had a heart for all the people in the camp, not simply for his own congregation. We also tried to discern which one of the pastors would not draw attention to himself or use his role to recruit people for his church or for his brand of theology.

We needed a servant-leader.

However, there was a language barrier. Not all of the pastors spoke English, so the communication was strained even with an interpreter present. However, words are not required for a humble countenance to shine through the verbal limitations.

After all had spoken, Dr. Finegan and I knew we had found our man – Pastor Sincere. Like the other pastors, he too lost family members. However, the humble spirit of this man was evident to all. We sensed that Pastor Sincere was a suffering servant who could lead the other pastors, that he was the right man for selfless leadership. This was a God-moment for both Dr. Finegan and me.

We thanked and dismissed the other pastors and met with Pastor Sincere for a couple of hours to develop a message that he could teach the other pastors. Our strategy was to train the local pastors to deliver an evidenced-based presentation about how God had worked in their own history and to cast a vision for a better future so as to stimulate the people's hope.

"God was with us in the past and is with us now." This vision statement was simple and the pastors agreed to the message. These local pastors would use their country's own history of tragedies and oppression as concrete examples of God working.

There was a strategic corner in the camp area that was ideal as a makeshift outdoor amphitheater. It had a little stage with lights and stadium speakers thanks to the military and their generators. The speakers were powerful enough to be heard 500 feet away. Pastors took turns each evening addressing the throngs. The people gathered at sundown and the message was delivered. Their preaching style had a rhythmic cadence:

"Remember this tragedy? ... God was with us.

Remember that dictator? ... God was with us.

Remember the earthquakes? ... God was with us."

Then they spoke of present examples. They reminded the people that the day after the tsunami, food arrived. Day two, water was delivered. Then the third day, God produced the medical and disaster teams. "God is at work again."

As the people listened to their trusted clergymen, they had reason to hope again. For all their suffering, these people had resiliency, a high capacity to bounce back.

The pastors embraced their own pain and now were empowered to hold the people's suffering as well. When they stood up, they spoke with power and authority, with a fierce courage. When they declared, "God is with us…", the people believed and felt hope.

Fierce Courage and Midnight Courage are contagious and empowering.

Report 24   Singing and Suffering

That night, after meeting with the pastors and Pastor Sincere, I wrote the following entry into my journal:

"We have 50,000 homeless people. There is not one square of toilet paper in the whole camp and the sanitary conditions are dangerous. The people are peaceful, calmed by the local pastors we enlisted to help with that task.

"Our medical clinic delivered our second baby. The mother named the baby Sam, after Uncle Sam. A nurse suggested, "How about Samantha? You have a baby girl." This was incredibly inspiring. I am so blessed to witness these human extremes of birth and death."

On Wednesday morning at about 4:30 a.m., I got up and stood by the edge of the camp. Beside me were a dozen Army Rangers who stood guard over the slumbering camp. The night sky was so crystal clear that the stars felt close enough to touch and I envisioned wandering spirits bouncing from star to star like a giant pinball game.

Off to my right, about 200 feet away, the quiet of the night was broken by three or four voices singing a tune I did not recognize. In seconds, fifty more joined in and the only word I could catch was "Hallelujah."

Hallelujah or Alleluia are universal words, understood and used in most every language. Their song or hymn seemed akin to our "Amazing Grace" in that everyone knew it. Soon, five hundred voices blended in, followed by thousands more. Within forty-five seconds 50,000 singers had taken up the melody!

They raised their voices to heaven in unison, and the force of their singing left no one a passive observer. Soldiers on the line, slung their M-16 rifles over their shoulders so they could raise their arms in praise. I felt my arms stretching toward heaven as well.

With the eyes of faith, I saw earthbound voices rise into a heavenly choir, lifting up and up into the night sky. Heaven stirred. Then it was as if a Hand came down from Heaven and hovered gently over the camp, giving comfort and grace for the new day of suffering and dying that would soon begin at sunrise. After about three minutes, the voices began to fall off and soon it was quiet again.

I confess that I am using inadequate, weak human language in the attempt to describe a truly spiritual event. I believe that we witnessed a visitation of Biblical proportions.

Afterward, I experienced a paradox of two strong reactions. First, I felt humbled. These people had almost nothing before the earthquake one week ago, and now even what they did have was taken away. Before me was a population trained in suffering, and this morning they were singing. These dear people were demonstrating how a person can suffer deeply and still have joy to sing.

Inspired was my second reaction. I thought I was bringing God to these people, but the Lord was already with them. God was here moving among them on that early morning. I was profoundly inspired by the people's patience and endurance while surviving in rubble and squalor. I hope I will remember to sing the next time I suffer.

We had taught the local pastors to give the message, *God is with us*, but on this night I saw that Heaven was already working among them. Although they had suffered deep poverty and cruel oppression, they knew that God was with them!

Report 25   Atrocities As A Lifestyle

I was bursting with joy at surveying the results of 110 years of sacrificial work by the Presbyterian Church in South Sudan, which at the time, was the newest country in the world. There were dozens of schools, sanitation systems, clean water sites, hospitals... until they were destroyed.

Pastor Oruzu reported an armed attack on his village, Pibor, by a rival tribe that killed over eight hundred of Pastor Oruzu's clan who were mostly Presbyterians. That part is horrible, but what made this particular event so horrendous for me was that the slaughter was carried out by a tribe who were also Presbyterians, my own denomination! How could this happen?

"They carried AK-47s in one hand and Bibles in the other," Pastor Oruzu reported. Then the assailants had a prayer meeting after they attacked Pibor, thanking God for this victory. The assault was made more outrageous by occurring on Christmas Eve, the day before most Christians celebrate the birth into our world of Jesus Christ, the Prince of Peace.

Prior to our traveling to Pibor, we sought intel on what to expect from an area located in a rebel-contested area. A respected American, Bill Andress, had visited Pibor many times because it was the "poorest of the poor."

He referred me to an American named Laurie who had started an orphanage there and could give me the latest information. In a phone conversation with her, she described herself as a young, fair-complexioned, single woman from South Carolina who had felt the calling to help orphans in South Sudan. I asked her to describe her work.

"I went to Pibor, found a suitable home and started caring for orphans." It was a loving and ambitious accomplishment. "But", she continued, "rebels surrounded my place and began shooting their AK-47s in the air – for an hour!"

Laurie knew she would be raped and feared the same or worse for the children. Instead, she hoped she would just be killed first. However, during a lull when the rebels were reloading, this brave young woman escaped with the children.

I can only imagine the fear and relief she must have felt at her successful escape. She made it safely back to the U.S. and immediately went into trauma counseling. However, she would not be deterred. A year later she returned to Pibor and opened another orphanage.

Orphans do not have access to any type of counseling and these types of violence are standard fare where they live. How do they manage to survive with this level of "normal"?

Having heard many similar stories about life in Sudan, I do not allow women on these high risk missions. Many local men view women as rape fodder.

When I returned home, I gave a report on my work in Sudan to a church. After the session, a woman begged me to go on our next trip. I tried to dissuade her, but she was determined to join my team.

She seemed inspired by the challenges I had described and insisted that I tell her the "worst that could happen." Sooooooo… I told her.

"Well, there is something I have not told you," I began. "When we land in Juba, I will hand you two condoms." I paused to let this sink in. "You will use them for bargaining." Again, I paused. Initially she just stared at me. Then her expression changed to disbelief and finally to disgust. I continued, "You will tell your attackers that you will not resist them – if they use the condom."

"I would NEVER submit," she said defiantly. "I would fight, tear his eyes out and rip his balls off." I did not see that one coming from a church lady!

"Hmmm." I acknowledged, "Well, that is one approach." I chose not to debate her. "However, they have the weapons and we may not be able to protect you." Taking an American white woman to these rebel-held areas is not only dangerous for her, but it also raised the level of risk for the rest of the team.

"They will separate you from us... They will rape you and you will probably get AIDS." My statement sounded like a death notification: clear, direct truth.

So, why offer the condoms? "If they choose not to kill you, at least you will have some protection from contracting AIDS." The church lady lost interest.

I chose not to tell her that one Sudanese soldier boasted to me that he had a special way to get rid of AIDS: "Have sex with a virgin." He was serious. "A five year old is the best," he added. I gave him an incredulous look.

Report 26   Procedures vs. People

At another site, people had been forced out of their homes taking nothing with them – no extra clothing, food, water or medications. They were taken to one of the hastily assembled shelters and at first they were thankful to be alive. Hundreds of people needed medical care and made their way to our medical clinic.

Members of gangs also fled to our shelter. On their way they had broken into gun stores and were now armed, dangerous and drug-seeking. Our situation was frightening.

Wandering, marauding gangs threatened to overrun our clinic to confiscate our supply of medications. They believed we had narcotics. We found ourselves caught in an extremely dangerous predicament.

"Are we going to make it out of here alive?" asked Mark, a paramedic team member.

"The Lord is with us," I answered, but I did not know if the Lord would rescue us or not.

In the chaos and danger, we received an urgent message from a credible authority that our clinic was in imminent danger of being overrun and that we should flee immediately. Unlike those who were confined inside the earlier-mentioned large stadium and not allowed to leave, our team was in a position to escape. Then the shooting started.

In our scramble toward safety, we were forced to abandon all of our belongings, which included personal treasures and prescription medications. For me, the personal loss included my 45 year-old Bible, my personal journal of 35 years and all of my prescription medications.

I take one medication for Attention Deficit Hyperactivity Disorder and one for an excruciatingly painful restless leg condition that feels as if I am being struck with cattle prods all night long. I would not lose my life without my medications, but several of my teammates needed their prescriptions for serious, life-threatening conditions.

After we fled for our lives and were in a secure place, our pharmacist, Julie, surveyed the team to prepare a list of the team's lost personal prescriptions. Her hope was to get them replaced before any health crises presented themselves. Julie and I went in search of the gentleman whose job it was to restock our pharmaceuticals in the clinic.

When we found him, Julie explained what had happened and handed him the list of medications. She fully expected he would grasp our predicament and quickly replenish our missing medications.

"It's impossible to accommodate your request," he replied. "It's not my responsibility to replace the medications you lost." Then he added, "Next time, don't leave them behind."

"What!" We were stunned. He was not going to help us.

"These aren't luxuries or extravagances," Julie replied. "They are necessary for sustaining the team members' health!"

Julie is a genuinely nice and extremely competent lady. She took the reasonable approach with this man, but it was not producing positive results. She stood there stunned. She was at a loss for how to proceed.

I was thinking of all the threats and harsh words I could use to light a fire under him to make him do the right thing and help us. There are limits to being nice. Sometimes the prophet needs to threaten stubborn people with the judgment fire of God.

I opened my mouth to ask his name, pulling out a pen and notepad to record it. If he asked why, I was going to tell him, "So we would know whom to sue afterwards when our people have problems because you refused to get us medications!"

Without my saying a word, his countenance changed. I was not sure if God had performed a miracle that suddenly softened his heart or if the man just snapped out of his brain numbing bureaucratic training.

In an about-face, he said, "Well, let's see what we can do." He turned around, stepped to a file cabinet and pulled open one of the drawers. He removed a folder, pulled out a reimbursement form and handed it to Julie.

"Take this to a local pharmacy and they will fill your prescriptions." Perhaps this gentleman had a God-moment or perhaps his empathetic humanity kicked in. Whatever the case, we picked up the prescriptions and everyone on our team was thankful.

I caught a glimpse of and understood how the evacuees must be viewing us, as they suffered under our procedures – procedures that were meant to speed treatments and keep order.

All of us have the choice whether or not to do the right thing when we are faced with so many opportunities to choose the wrong. The formerly rigid official who for a time would not or could not abandon the safety line of "following orders" easily could have chosen to stand his ground, but fortunately, he chose to help us.

An example that tragically illustrates the chasm between following procedures vs. taking care of people occurred in one world-class disaster that required "all hands" to help. I stood next to a First Responder Physician from Boston, Dr. Mark

Pearlmutter.[10]

He knelt over a woman who was gasping for air as he

treated her for a severe breathing complication. I watched him

skillfully keep her alive with chest compressions when a soldier

walked up to us.

"I'm sorry, but you must stop what you are doing and leave

now," he ordered. The doctor turned his head, still tending his

patient, and looked up at the young man issuing orders.

"What?" asked the confused doctor.

"You are not licensed to practice medicine in this state and

you must stop at once." Dr. Pearlmutter was caught off guard. I

just stood there in shock at the conversation.

"What?" the doctor repeated. He had heard him correctly;

he just could not process it. "Can I at least care of her until a

local doctor can come and tend to her?" he appealed. "If I leave

now, she will most certainly die."

"I'm sorry. You must leave now," the man insisted. It was

evident from the soldier's expression that he was miserable

over being the messenger of this bad news. Apparently he was

following orders issued from way above his level.

---

10 Dr. Mark Pearlmutter tells his own story:
http://rense.com/general67/doctorsaysFEMAordered.htm

Dr. Pearlmutter turned his face back to the woman. He paused for a moment trying to comprehend that he was ordered to leave. Slowly, he uncurled his long body, rose to his feet, paused again and walked away.

It appeared that the bureaucracy was consumed by the risk of liability. However, working at a disaster site carries risk. Avoiding the risk of liability carried more benefits than preventing death.

I cannot describe the depth of anger that Dr. Pearlmutter and I felt at the enforcement of a rule that forbade the use of common sense and compassion.

When Karl Menninger, psychiatrist and author of *The Crime of Punishment,* was asked, "What do you do when ethics conflict?"

"Do whatever is most human,"[11] he answered.

I thank God that the leaders and commanders that I serve under are tested, responsible, brave souls who combine the best of professional emergency skills... and common sense.

---

11 Menninger, Karl, The Crime of Punishment, AuthorHouse, October 3, 2007.

Report 27   When Right Feels Wrong

Some choices are complicated. I have made enough poor choices over the years to be cautious when I am convinced that this time I am right! Someone observed, "Being right is just about as dangerous a position as any of us can find ourselves in." The two following incidents illustrate when right seems wrong.

After Typhoon Hainan razed the coastline of the Philippines with a 30-foot tidal surge, I joined a small team whose mission was to hand deliver livelihood tools to help survivors, especially the poorest of the survivors. We did not bring food, water, or nails because of their bulk and weight.

These energetic people needed fishing tools so they could catch fish to eat and to reestablish their livelihoods. Fishing poles, tackle gear, nets and boats were swept away... along with their means of providing food for their families. In our backpacks, we carried hundreds of fishhooks.

Spread among our backpacks were over a hundred rechargeable solar panels to give to widows, who were especially economically vulnerable in their social structure.

Because of the widows' age and health, they were not economic producers and were thus marginalized by the community.

At each village, we sought out a widow and gave her a solar recharger and a means to make an income. Villagers would pay her to recharge their cell phones and batteries. With a solar charger she became indispensable to her community.

While moving through a debris field that was once a crowded village, we came upon a woman picking through the rubble that was once her home. Like so many others in the area, she appeared to be rummaging to recover useable items. Rev. Jeanie Shaw, one of our disaster pastor teammates, stepped over rubble and struck up a conversation with her.

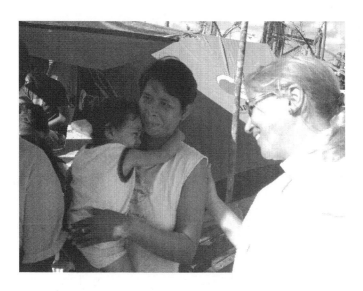

Rev. Jeanie Shaw, a Disaster Pastor, comforts a mother

"I am searching for my 18 month old daughter," the woman explained. She was able to save her other four children from the 200 mile an hour winds and torrential water. But, her infant daughter "was ripped out of my arms." Jeanie's heartstrings were pulled and she wanted to help this mother.

"Can we help this mother find her missing child?" Jeanie asked our team leader, Dan Johanson, a missionary in the Philippines. Dan was faced with a tough choice.

"No," he said after considerable discussion with the team. "We need to move on to a new area." His reasoning? Dan explained that we could spend all day digging through the debris and still not find the child. "Our primary task is to help the living, not the dead." The child could easily have been swept 100 feet away and buried under several feet of debris. With conflicted thoughts we left the area and the woman who was continued her search alone.

What makes these kinds of decisions so complicated depends on each individual's values, worldview and temperament. Dan's reasoning used impenetrable logic and it came from his head. The reasoning of those who wanted to help the mother was based on deeply held, non-negotiable values arising from their hearts.

Dan Johanson works with a fishing village called Bajao.[12]

We moved on to where there were numbers of desperate people who were alive and in great need. In disasters, leaders are often called upon to make tough decisions. Dan's was logical and mission-focused, but some felt it was cruel. Neither position was right or wrong per se.

Often conflict emerges when opposing positions are trying to occupy the same space. After Dan listened carefully to everyone's opinion he made the decision to move on. He was the responsible leader and we had the responsibility to follow him.

These kinds of conflicts often feel strange, the ones where the right thing feels wrong. I witnessed this when I was a

---

[12] Information can be found at BadjaoBridge.org

teenager, growing up on Marine Corps bases. Living on a military base is remarkably safe for kids. Despite all of the weapons, fighting machines and amped-up testosterone, shootings were rare, no home invasions or kidnappings.

However, living on a Marine Corps Air Facility had routines that were different from civilian towns. There were the ever-present sights and sounds of jets or assault helicopters taking off or of heavy transports landing.

Actually, these were so routine that we tuned them out and treated them like back ground noise; sort of like city kids ignoring honking cars or wailing sirens. While this was interesting, it was still routine.

Report 28   Disastrous Routines

In the summer, I could usually be found with our family's ski boat, water-skiing on the river; or, I was at the boat dock about a half-mile from our house in the officers' quarters. There, boat owners would launch and retrieve their boats from a spacious cement boat ramp.

One afternoon we stopped early because the wind picked up and the water became too choppy to ski. We pulled our ski boat out of the water onto a trailer and my dad towed it home. I wanted to help others get their boats out of the water, so I stayed behind.

All afternoon one or two helicopters flew slow circles about 5,000 feet above the airfield. This was an ordinary, routine sight for Saturday afternoons. Helicopter engines had to be replaced at regular intervals and were often tested on Saturdays when there was little traffic on the runway. Helicopter pilots would get bored orbiting the airfield, so they made the space available for several paratroopers who would practice jumping.

With nothing happening on the boat ramp, I looked up and saw two paratroopers standing at an open door of a helicopter for a moment and then jump. The routine was that their shoots opened immediately and they made a leisurely descent to a landing spot on a large open field at the end of the runway.

However, on this Saturday, I could tell that something was wrong.

The gusty winds carried both men horizontally over my head and a mile out over the river. Within a minute, I watched them set down in the water. Without an immediate rescue, they would easily become entangled in their soaked parachute lines and be pulled down to the bottom.

I wished I still had the family ski boat in the water. I knew that my father and I undoubtedly would take off after these two fellows. It was obvious what had to be done.

I was helpless to rescue them. This was a life and death situation for them. Every second counted.

The only boat still in the water was a heavy 12-passenger transport vessel used to ferry personnel the three miles between the Main Base and the Air Facility. Minutes passed. Eventually, a corporal who normally operated the boat strolled out, stepped into the boat and started the launch procedures.

I had seen him do this ordinary routine many times and felt a powerful mixture of relief, hope and dread. Relief, because someone was finally going to rescue the two men. However, my hope quickly turned to dread.

His protocol included leisurely warming up the engine, then walking along the deck casting the lines free. This procedure would take at least 12 minutes. To the drowning men, that was a lifetime.

Running up and down the boat dock, I shouted in panic at the driver, "go ... Go," and finally screaming as loud as I was able, *"GO!"* If I were an officer, I would have ordered him to forget the warm up routine and immediately head out to rescue the drowning men.

After what felt like an eternity, the transport driver finally pulled away from the dock and headed at a trolling speed towards the two men in the water. To get a better view, I ran to a small knoll to watch what would happen.

I could see one paratrooper flailing in deeper water about 200 feet from the shoreline. Tangled in the cords of his parachute, he struggled against its weight that pulled him down like an anchor.

Several times I watched as his head popped to the surface to gulp air and then go under once more. The other paratrooper stood waist deep on a shoal near a beach. He was safe.

Initially, the rescue boat headed for the paratrooper who was in deeper water and struggling for his life. But, at the last moment, the driver diverted his boat to first rescue the paratrooper who was safe on the shoal.

After wasting several minutes carefully maneuvering the boat to pick up the safe paratrooper, the driver then turned the boat around to rescue the struggling Marine in deeper water.

By the time the rescue boat arrived, all they found was part of a parachute floating on the surface. The two men in the boat pulled the parachute onboard until they found the other paratrooper – drowned, dead. I watched them pull his lifeless body up out of the water and into the boat.

Then my hope and dread turned into an overwhelming fury. Never had I experienced such extreme anxiety that now combined a powerful rage. There was nothing I could do but watch helplessly. I wanted revenge on that inept transit driver.

Why? Because the driver blindly followed his warm up procedures while a young Marine died unnecessarily. The transit driver's rigidity in following procedures that were meant for normal times were totally inappropriate in a crisis.

In my mind, he was utterly negligent not to adapt. This life and death crisis should have alerted him to use an alternative procedure. I wish I could have convinced him to suspend his regular procedures when seconds counted and lives could be lost. Ever since that day, when I see a rule or procedure that jeopardizes people unnecessarily, I seethe inside with involuntary anger.

Looking back, I am still deeply persuaded that I was right, that the driver should have suspended his warm-up procedures when a life was at stake. I am still convinced of it to this day and it has settled inside of me as one of my deeply-held values: "People take priority over procedures."

However, I asked Dave, a wise, highly experienced and deeply respected First Responder to read this paratrooper story. His professional perspective disagrees with mine yet I confess his reaction is reasoned and makes sense.

He wrote:

"This story struck me in perhaps a very different way than you intended it to. Professional rescuers know and are taught that the rescuer's safety comes before that of the victim. At the firehouse, we always took time to gear-up, acknowledge the dispatcher, turn off the stove, etc., no matter what the call was for.

"There may be times when an experienced crew can take some shortcuts, but I can easily understand the military perspective of "don't ever change the launch procedure" because soldiers and Marines tend to be young, brash and inexperienced – they could too easily make judgment errors that would violate the "rescuer safety comes first" paradigm.

"Even the 'which person to rescue first' can be viewed differently. To maximize outcome, it may be standard practice to 'rescue the easy victims first.' Or, perhaps the operator didn't see the situation the way you could/did from the shore. Or perhaps it was operator inexperience rather than a question 'procedure vs. people.'

"To me, this story conveys the challenges of 'the lay public doesn't understand the technicalities of emergency response'. I can see how the story could generate a negative reaction from professional rescuers."

I have learned to listen carefully to other voices, especially when I think I am right. As previously stated, "thinking that we are right is just about as dangerous a position as any of us can find ourselves in."

Report 29   Listening To The Local Citizens

One of my passions is training groups how to be ready to survive a disaster. Through the media, we hear of disasters here and around the world, but most people know little about adequately preparing for them nor do they receive training to be a volunteer if a disaster occurs in their area. Perhaps it is our denial mechanism at work, but it seems that as soon as a disaster is off the news, we forget to prepare ourselves for future disasters.

A common occurrence I see is that the news and talk shows create a pool of "experts". Usually they are from national or international organizations, but rarely are they local. Those with local experience, knowledge, and wisdom need to have their voices heard when a disaster strikes.

Unfortunately, people with local memories and wisdom, those who know the culture and idiosyncrasies of the area where the disaster is occurring, who remember what has worked and not worked in their community, are often marginalized and ignored by the "outside experts".

For example, during one disaster, a local volunteer named Tammy Searle immediately reported to a large local shelter and volunteered to help. As a gifted organizer, she quickly saw there was no system or management of the victims, resources or other volunteers... just pandemonium and chaos.

Tammy Searle

Tammy[13] had eyes to see that a food court needed to be placed by a water source; sleeping areas needed to be set up in a quiet part of the building, medical screening and registration would be better placed by the front door.

She recruited six young Mormon missionaries stranded at the shelter and recruited them to set up folding tables and chairs. She found an RN to gather medical supplies to treat people and drafted eight church ladies to prepare feeding stations.

---

[13] http://tammyandfriends.com

She experienced first hand many Divine Appointments. "I felt that God was everywhere," she confessed. I asked her to tell me more.

"God appeared through so may volunteers and people donating goods." She recalled one incident of a lady who had "bales and bales of hay to donate but it was in Northern California and had no means of transporting it to the fairgrounds." Tammy politely asked her to wait to see if she could find transportation.

Tammy was excited to tell me what happened. "The very next person that walked up to me said he had a semi-trailer to transport anything needed. This gentleman walked up from a completely opposite direction. He was not privy to my previous conversation with the woman. That is divine intervention." God worked through Tammy in this manner for days and many more prayers were answered in this manner.

Tammy noticed many children at the Fairgrounds and her motherly instincts kicked in. She turned the top level of the building into a fun place for the kids. Televisions, toys, art supplies and the like were donated. A few of the kids created artwork for Tammy as a way to thank her and created a banner and declared their area, "Camp Tammy". Kids actually enjoyed their time at the shelter.

She remembered, "details are often overlooked in times of crisis. However, if you are fortunate enough to have volunteers, details can be addressed."

She gave an example. "When people came to the fairgrounds they went through the serpentine of tables with donations upon them. They were asked if they specifically left something behind that they now needed."

"This one little girl said, 'My Dora toothbrush.'" Tammy made a mental note of this little detail. A short while later a Dora toothbrush came in; she made sure that the little girl received it.

Everyone came to the shelter: rich and homeless, able bodied and the infirmed. "A few of the older folks were very nervous that they had brought items of high value to the shelter." What to do?

"There were Armed National Guard setting up and assisting in many ways." She got the soldiers to mingle in the area where she located the elderly. The young soldiers and the elderly began to chat and play cards.

One lady told Tammy, "The service I received here at the shelter was equal to the Four Seasons." This was a lady that a few days prior was extremely nervous about being there as she had heard so many horror stories from Katrina.

Afterwards, Tammy reported to me several Lessons Learned. "People realized they could live without so many possessions which made them realize how emotionally draining so many material possessions can create upon us."

On a personal level, Tammy said, "we can still be happy while displaced from our normal routine. We can learn to 'let go' of so many possessions as they are not a direct reflection of our personal worth."

This crisis created new trust levels that did not exist before. "Many different socio-economic groups were all put into the same area," Tammy reported, "and surprise, surprise they all got along as fellow human beings — stereotypes were dropped and different castes were melded together."

Tammy has an irresistible personality and people recognized her common sense and organizational skills, so they followed her gifted leadership.

Though untrained, Tammy possessed the best qualities of a professional Incident Commander. Mike Hillmann, a disaster expert and writer, describes characteristics of anyone in charge at a disaster:

"The effective incident commander must be: calm in the face of danger; focused; possess the ability to prioritize; have a positive attitude; be decisive and relentless in achieving objectives; apply experience from prior assignments; be able to set aside his or her ego; be in good physical condition; have the ability to overcome obstacles; and anticipate/manage change."[14] That was Tammy.

Then we, an outside disaster medical team, with our incredibly competent team commander, arrived. He observed that Tammy had set up a smooth-running shelter. Rather than insisting on doing things our way, he wisely decided that we would come alongside her system and assist with medical services. This cooperative partnership worked fine, but it did not last.

The following day, a nationally recognized relief organization arrived and insisted that they would take over the whole operation and run it their way – the established way, "the right way." In an ugly confrontation, Tammy was forced off the site, local volunteers were dismissed and a mountain of donated resources was hauled to the landfill. Unbelievable!

Regrettably, those managers had only one playbook with mandated checklists. They could not adapt nor partner with a local system that was already in place and working well. Rather than leaving an empowered community of local workers for the

---

[14] Cynthia Renaud, "The Missing Piece of NIMS: Teaching Incident Commanders How to Function in the Edge of Chaos." *Homeland Security Affairs* 8, Article 8 (June 2012), http://www.hsaj.org/?article-8.1.8

long-range recovery effort, dispirited volunteers left with a bitter experience and were no longer available.

The better scenario is for the professionals and locals to join together in bringing all the resources available and distribute them for the benefit of the victims and the community.

The truth is, outside agencies and relief workers always arrive after the fact; the disaster has already occurred. So, in reality, locals are actually the First Responders.

Report 30   Listening to Local Heroes

Eight thousand miles from Tammy, I met a pastor, James
Tut (pronounced Toot), who served as the leader of pastors and
the Presbyterian churches in the Islamic Republic of Sudan, the
northern part of the former country of Sudan, which had
suffered a terrible civil war at the cost of millions of lives.

Warlords, like Joseph Kony, became famous for kidnapping
young males (an estimated 66,000) and turning them into "Boy
Soldiers". You will not hear of this place because it is too
hazardous for reporters or cameras to go. Terrorists like Osama
bin Laden started his monstrous crusade here. In 2013, the
country divided into two nations with Muslims in the north and
Christians in the south.

Sudan is the darkest and scariest place in the world. This
is where I take my little light.

The Presbyterian Church paid for Tut's theological
education and he returned to his ethnic community as a
pastor. To me, Pastor Tut displayed amazing courage when he
left his former state religion, but he blushed when I called him a
hero.

"I will tell you about heroes," he said. He reported that
hundreds of members from his tribe started following Jesus

through his ministry. He raised up several dozen pastors who courageously serve their people.

Rev. James Tut

I felt like a student in the presence of a legendary master. Pastor Tut succeeded in the kind of mission work that often resulted in tribal rivalry and an old-fashioned stoning.

"We heard about a village that was starving in a war-torn area," he began. Food deliveries were regularly confiscated by rebels and the village had not received supplies in many days.

Tut and a few of his brave friends loaded a dump truck

with food and made the dangerous trip to deliver life-giving supplies to the famished people. However, even in these dire circumstances, some of the villagers were reluctant to receive the food because "it was offered by people of a different tribe".

"Go ask the Tribal Chief," Tut suggested, having no idea what he would recommend. So, the people asked, "Can we eat the food offered by an enemy tribe?"

"Who are the real enemy?" the Chief asked his people. "Your Boy Soldiers destroyed your villages and murdered your families. Are they feeding you? These people are offering you food. Go, eat!"

"We serve the people, then they listen to us," he repeated several times. But outreach had come at a dear price. "It is not safe to be a Christian where I live (in northern Sudan). Many pastors I know have been stoned to death."

Report 31   Listening To Local Solutions

We traveled about twenty-five long miles over the worst road conditions I have ever seen. Our journey was from the South Sudan capitol of Juba to a refugee camp called Gorome. It was established specifically for the Ethiopians who had managed to escape from their own country. The roads to Gorome were bumpy, deeply rutted and full of potholes the size of bomb craters.

The drawback of these almost impassable roads, is that they make the camps virtually inaccessible and isolated from all resources - food, clothing, medical supplies, water - everything. The benefit of these disastrous roads is that the refugee camp is less accessible to those perpetuating genocide in Ethiopia.

The Camp Director at Gorome, a highly honored man named Pakwan steered us through a military checkpoint and called our attention to the people being tortured. Yes! Bludgeoned right in front of us.

Soldiers stood over hunched bodies, beating the daylights out of defenseless people. Why? They did not have the proper papers. Of course they had no papers!

They had fled their homes and were running for their lives, barely a step ahead of the murderous soldiers. After such severe suffering, those that escaped were finally allowed inside the Gorome Refugee Camp, where most will remain for the rest of their lives.

The Ethiopian government butchered at least 1.4 million of its own citizens.[15] Why were they killing their own people? I cannot and probably will never understand. Men and women told me horrifying stories of torture and murders of family members and friends.

Several described how the Chinese government had purchased enormous tracks of Ethiopian ancestral land that the Chinese now use for farming. After the sale, the Ethiopian authorities declared that the local citizens were squatters on Chinese land and forcibly removed them from their ancestral land with nowhere else to settle.

Injustice is the issue. Women and children are especially vulnerable. Writing in *The Hole in our Gospel*, the President of World Vision, Richard Stearns, concurs with what we have witnessed. "Widows have their land confiscated by bullying male relatives; girls are raped or forced into prostitution; money lenders prey upon children through bonded labor; corrupt

---

15 Valentino, Benjamin A. (2004). *Final Solutions:* Mass Killing and Genocide in the Twentieth Century. Ithaca: Cornell University Press. p. 196.

governments embezzle the money meant to build school and clinics."[16]

One young Ethiopian man showed me a hand-drawn map he had used as he hiked twenty-three days through thick brush to reach this camp in South Sudan.

A young woman, about eighteen, entered the camp with scratches all over her body after having walked three weeks through the brush, only to discover that her two girlfriends had been captured by soldiers. She may never know what evil befell them.

Numerous refugees showed me wounds and scars on their arms and backs, blows to their heads, all evidence of severe beatings. They needed to show someone and tell their stories, hoping somehow that by reporting their stories, hoping that their experiences would influence the sane world to come to their aid and rescue them.

When Ethiopian child-refugees arrived in the camp, they attended classes in reading, English, Math, Science and Christian Education. The only resources that teachers have are old-fashioned black chalkboards. No books, no paper, no pencils. Somehow, the teachers educate these children, as it has been

---

[16] Richard Stearns, *The Hole in our Gospel*, Thomas Nelson publishers, 2009, p. 127.

said... doing so much with so little and occasionally doing the impossible with nothing!

Hundreds of these precious little children surrounded my two partners and me. We discovered that taking their pictures was a big thrill for them, providing a little joy in their otherwise bleak environment. Many children looked puzzled at our white skin and touched our hands and arms.

I joined a dozen men, sitting in the shade like a pride of lions under an African savanna tree. To think of myself as a lion made me sit a little taller as I imagined myself fluffing my imaginary mane.

I asked the men to tell me their stories, anticipating some would be awful, some joyful, perhaps even some humorous. I was nowhere near prepared for what they told me.

I learned that many of the men had multiple wives, but more importantly, I learned why. It had nothing to do with male prowess, machismo desires or any type of a sense of male dominance.

Having multiple wives was a practical solution to a common problem: a widow with children needed protection that only a husband can provide in this culture. If widows remain unmarried, they are vulnerable to rape, robbery or to any of the depraved acts of men.

The dozen men sitting around me had multiple wives and other men's children, which to me was sacrificial to its core. One gentleman in his late sixties had twenty-three children and three wives. Another a younger man, Otto, had fourteen children and two wives.

I came to the sober conviction that having multiple wives was their safety net solution, a social accommodation resulting from so many slaughtered husbands and fathers.

In the Old Testament, the prophet Isaiah observed a similar accommodation for his time:

"And in that day seven women shall take hold of one man, saying, 'We will eat our own bread, and wear our own apparel: only let us be called by your name, to take away our reproach.'" Isaiah 4:1.

Although I am not used to the idea of multiple wives, I now finally understand the necessity for it and accept it as self-giving rather than self-serving.

Report 32   Listening To Mosquitoes

From my journal written in the middle of the night:

"Even in broad daylight, this camp carries a darkness that can be felt. Then, when the sun retreats over the horizon and genuine darkness covers the land, it hides the worst of all predators: mosquitoes! I have not slept more than one hour tonight. A squadron of mosquitoes made coordinated attacks on me without mercy. I have searched for a word or phrase to accurately portray the vast swarms of these tiny predators, but it fails me."

Imagine thousands of marauding mosquitos, where one in 73 carry malaria, and here I am with no netting or repellent.

It was a little late to reflect back on the conversation I had with two Africans who assured me, "No one uses netting or DEET at our camp." Really? Later, I would learn why: "Because there is no money for netting or DEET, not because they are not needed!"

This camp is so poor that people cannot afford the $2.00 for a net. Recently, I read in the *Proceedings of the National Academy of Sciences*, of research published by the University of California, Davis, that malaria-laden and insecticide-resistant "super mosquitos" can survive exposure to poisons meant to kill them.[17]

It is a little past 4:00 a.m. and I am exhausted…deep into depletion. I cannot think of a word that reflects how deeply worn out I am. Physically spent, mentally off-balance, emotionally numb, and I have no time to renew my run down self.

The final solution is to surrender my body to the mosquitoes… a big mistake on my part. Sleep overcomes me. Hoping they did not carry diseases was like wishing on the candles of past birthday cakes. Sleep did not last long.

During a snoring session I opened my mouth and swallowed a big mosquito! As it buzzed in the back of my throat, I sat up coughing, choking and spitting; anything to get it out of my mouth. I sent the tip of my tongue in search of the obnoxious insect, but the mosquito retreated further down my esophagus. I swatted my neck involuntarily and twisted my head to no avail.

Now, I was awake.

As soon as I returned home, I would pay for my lethargy by spending for a week in Stanford University Medical Center's Infectious Diseases ward while research doctors did tests to determine why my face was so grotesquely swollen, misshapen and bright red. Normal features on my face were

---

[17] www.pnas.org/content/early/2015/01/02/1418892112

unrecognizable and my family said I looked like a genetic mutant.

After a week doctors determined that a mosquito had infected my face with streptococcus and my sinuses with aspergilla.

Once they had names for the mysterious bugs that were destroying my body, they knew how to treat the threatening menace. They administered the correct antibiotics and healing came quickly.

Report 33   Listening To Warlords

Warlords are gifted negotiators – they use an AK-47 instead of logic, reason or persuasive speech to make their point. Although their negotiation style is simple and direct, it is alien to those of us from Western cultures. In South Sudan the countryside is run by Warlords.

Prior to going to South Sudan, I met a CIA operator who gave me great advice. He had just returned from working with Warlords in Afghanistan. Meeting him was a Divine Appointment. I knew there would come a time when I would need to know this skill. I listened as if my life depended on it. It would.

"First," he said lifting up one finger, "find The Man … the one with the most blood on his hands." That translated into, "Find the man who has the most kills, is the most violent, the most feared and respected. He's in charge," the operator said. "This man knows how to control his turf, like a Don in the Mafia. When he gives an order, everyone complies; only a fool would disregard it."

Then, lifting up two fingers, he said, "After finding The Man, give him gold. With a sack of gold you can buy his assistance. Simple as that."

To me, it sounded as immoral as it did simple.

"You don't make friendships... you buy friendships," he added.

"Even if I gave him gold, how do I know I can trust him?" I asked.

It is useless to run "background checks" to verify which Warlords are the trustworthy ones. It is impossible and useless to do "due diligence" in the bush. Their way of doing business in South Sudan runs opposite to Western accounting methods. In fact, my accountant complained about my lack of appropriate documentation when I returned from South Sudan.

"I am not going to get a receipt from a Warlord," I would explain. This amused me, but not my CPA. My practice now is to bring small gifts of that precious metal and include a gold necklace for one of his wives.

"Trust him?" the operator laughed. "He is a Warlord! You can only trust him to be a Warlord."

"And what is that?" I asked naively. The Operator blinked his eyes in disbelief. I was still thinking in the Western model of accountability and transparency.

"Giving a Warlord gold helps finance his goals of more control," he answered. Warlords need money to pay the soldiers and buy weapons.

"How much?" I asked.

"Oh, usually there would be eight, maybe a dozen gold coins in a sock." I quickly calculated the value to be $10,000 to $15,000. There is no way I could buy those kinds of friends.

Was this an honorable way of doing business as a Disaster Pastor? Probably not, but the choice to take a more excellent way is not available.

In a similar manner, it is routine for NGOs and relief agencies to hire "technicals" to protect their warehouses and convoys. Technicals are rebel soldiers who will guard your property for hire. You either hire them or they will rob your supplies. Your choice.

Guards protect church attenders

We attended a university church in Nairobi Kenya and had to pass through three guards searching for guns and grenades by wanding us with handheld metal detectors. Churches are easy targets for Islamists who attend a service and will roll a grenade down the isle during worship. Churches that have guards tend not to get bombed.

Most people are not aware that mega churches in America will have a security team who quietly moves among the people. After a worship service they will stand within two steps of the

Senior Pastor or walk the parameter of the children's play ground. These teams are usually retired police officers who volunteer to serve as sheep dogs who protect the sheep from the wolves.

Did you know that more people are murdered in churches than in schools? Columbine, Sandy Hook and Virginia Tech grab the headlines but churches take more hits. When a gunman killed seven people, including the Pastor, at the Morris Brown African Methodist Episcopal Church, a 3,000 member congregation in Charleston, S.C. church, the eyes of church leaders across America were opened to their vulnerabilities.

For example, in 2012 there were 5 shootings in schools as compared to 115 in churches.[18] One year does not make a trend. As of this writing, since Columbine in 1999, there have been 267 killings in schools across America.[19] [20] How about churches?[21]

335!

When the problem of violence reaches a level that causes church leaders in American to act, they will consider the useful models of other countries. Traveling in many third world

---

[18] June 18, 2015 post in Christianity Today.
http://www.christianitytoday.com/gleanings/2015/june/several-reportedly-dead-after-shooting-at-historic-black-ch.html
[19] National Center for Educational Statistics.
https://nces.ed.gov/programs/crimeindicators/crimeindicators2011/tables/table_01_1.asp
[20] https://en.wikipedia.org/wiki/List_of_school_shootings_in_the_United_States#2010s
[21] http://www.carlchinn.com/Church_Security_Concepts.html

countries I have found that armed guards keep people safer than having no guards.

A routine sight around the world

When I visited a huge shopping mall in Manila, Philippines I noticed that armed guards sat in front of each store: Nike shoes, pharmacies, banks, grocery stores, bicycle shops, book stores, computer stores. I met a Police Commander and asked him how many sworn officers were on duty at that moment in the Mall.

"More than 300," he answered. In a similar size Mall in America there might be a dozen unarmed low paid security personnel. If something serious occurs, they would dial 911 and get real police on the scene.

Understandably, churches are resistant to consider armed security because they preach a deeply held conviction that we should be peacemakers. It appears inconsistent for peacemakers to carry deadly weapons.

A growing number of church leaders are willing to have a few trained and disciplined members to carry concealed weapons (CCW). These are usually retired law enforcement officers who are trained and disciplined in "shoot, no shoot scenarios". However, all members should be trained that "if they see something... say something!"

Eventually, churches in America will have to reconcile the apparent contradiction of being prepared to use violent means to protect the sheep-le (people who act like sheep) who hope to worship in peace.

In the Old Testament, Nehemiah was a leader rebuilding the defensive walls of Jerusalem. However, his project was threatened from local enemies. His solution had to feel like a paradox, even hypocritical.

"We prayed to our God and posted a guard...." Surely the work was slowed because "Those who carried materials did their work with one hand and held a weapon in the other...."[22]

Every week I ride with local police. I am paired with a sworn officer for a 2 to 4 hour ride. Together we make DUI stops, inspect movement in dark buildings and enter domestic conflicts. I follow the officer on foot pursuits, have joined a few

---

[22] Nehemiah 4.9 and 17 NIV

fights and been shot at. The Chief requires me to wear a bulletproof vest under my Police Chaplain's uniform.

A while ago a minister friend asked why I wore a vest. His question was more like a challenge to my spirituality and level of trust in God's hand of protection.

"Where is your faith? Don't you believe that the Lord will protect you?" he asked in the presence of other ministers. I thought for a moment.

"I have more faith that the Lord will protect me when I wear my vest," I answered.

Like Nehemiah's solution, people of faith must not be naïve when those with evil intent lurk nearby. David wrote a poem where he noted, "...the wicked man hunts down the weak, who are caught in the schemes he devises." Later in the same psalm he observed, "He lies in wait near the villages; from ambush he murders the innocent, watching in secret for his victims."[23]

These statements read like current news reports of mass shootings in churches, theaters and schools where the innocent gather. Leaders are confronted with these realities and are asking, "What level of protection should we provide our people?

On deployments I do not carry a weapon. I have to talk my way in and out of hazardous situations. The danger can be palpable, especially in countries torn by civil war. There, I have

---

[23] Psalm 10.2 and 8 NIV

no rights; no one will come to rescue me. My government says they will not ever negotiate with terrorists. It is abundantly clear to me that I am not cloaked in U.S. protection when I land in a foreign country.

Have I ever been in real danger? Several times. What seems like a safe situation can suddenly turn hazardous. At other times, I knowingly walk into dangerous situations because what I am trying to achieve is important.

More often there are unseen threats that require Midnight courage; I have to keep moving, remain calm and try to stay alive.

Some friends, along with my wife, have described me as fearless. Hardly. Like anyone else, I have fears. Fear is my constant companion: fear of not being able to help, fear of helping in the wrong way, fear of the unfamiliar, fear of uncertainties, and of course, fear of dying. This last one, though, is primal and very present when I walk into the presence of a Warlord.

Rev. John Chinyowa, General Acuil Madut (former Warlord was then made Chief Law Enforcement Commander of all Police) and me.

As it turns out, I have never met a Warlord that I did not like.

So, how do I put the prospect of death in its place so it does not paralyze me? This may sound strange but it works for me.

Whenever I go on a mission, I assume I will not come back.

Actually, it is freeing for me to settle up with death and proceed with the freedom that brings. Settling up with death calms me and helps me focus on the work.

I certainly don't have a death wish. I know my survival instinct is hardcore healthy. I don't intentionally put myself in harm's way, like running through the middle of a gunfight. I don't take unnecessary chances. However, I don't let risk interfere or get in the way of doing what is necessary.

To me, being consumed with anxiety over the possibility of death is a terrible distraction and a waste of energy. I remind myself of this fact: I am safer doing what God wants me to do rather than staying behind and believing I am safer at home.

Report 34   Listening For Courage

My father was a good example of how to deal with fear and death. He was the Commanding Officer of a squadron of Marine Corps pilots when I was fifteen.

"Dad, did you ever send men on suicide missions?" I asked.

He paused for a moment. My question was impertinent. It violated a family rule: Don't talk about death or any unpleasant subject. After all, he was in the death making business. I do not know who made up that rule, but we all understood it.

As soon as it was out of my mouth, I immediately regretted asking him about suicide missions. I had launched my mouth before checking in with my brain. But it was too late – like trying to get toothpaste back into the tube. However, after I put the words out into the air I was not to be deterred.

"Um, yes," he replied succinctly. I was more shocked than curious now—at that age, my moral compass was simple and clear . . . black and white. The very thought that my father sent other fathers into harm's way sullied my virtuous image of him.

I remember feeling very nervous and disturbed about his answer. Actually, I did not like his answer. I asked another question.

"Did some of them not make it back?" I asked, dreading what he might answer.

"Yes," he said. Family rule or not, he plucked a moral cord that felt dissonant in my incensed soul. I had to confront his wrongdoing; justice demanded it.

"Dad," I began in an indignant tone, "how could you knowingly send men to their deaths?" I was outraged that my father could be responsible for the deaths of young pilots. I was reckless and presumptuous! Without waiting for his answer, I accused him with another question.

"Why did those men go on suicide missions?" I demanded. Depending on his answer, my righteous anger was primed to condemn him for his immoral actions.

"I always led the mission," he stated.

That was the first God Moment in my memory. It changed my attitude, my opinion and my perspective on death. I am not cavalier about death, but I have been around it enough to know how, well, how final it is. While I do not fear death, I do not welcome it either.

Fear is a gift from God to alert me to danger. It must be managed, but I need enough of it to keep me alert.

I do have a lingering fear. It is that I will die before I am finished with my life's work, before my grandchildren grow up, before all of my prayers have been prayed.

I feel a deep heartfelt gratitude for the gift of my father, Marine Corps Major Herbert Nelson, who modeled fierce courage.   From his model I would learn how to turn towards chaos and darkness with my small light to bring consolation and encouragement to those who have experienced trauma and oppression.

Report 35   Life In A Refugee Camp

Several of the South Sudan refugee camps hold between 25,000 and 45,000 souls. A couple of them have over 100,000. On this trip, the task of getting to the refugee camp, Gorome, involved traveling about twenty-five miles through rebel-held territory.

We were thankful for the United Nations van with the bold, blue UN letters on it. The van offered only minimal protection, but it did provide some peace of mind for us. It was similar to the security I feel when I am wearing my Kevlar bulletproof vest while serving as a police chaplain back home.

There were plenty of checkpoints along the way. They operated like a mobster's bazaar. Imagine being forced to stop where street thugs, racketeers with guns, batons and brass knuckles shake down the vehicle occupants. These checkpoints are lawless places defined by who has the biggest gun. The one with the biggest gun makes the law.

Negotiating our way through the checkpoints was like sending a virgin teenage daughter to human traffickers for counseling. I soon discovered that this was nothing compared to the insides of the camps themselves.

The government in South Sudan forbade any refugee from being assimilated into the greater society because of the country's high unemployment rate for its own citizens. Rebels waited outside camps to rob, rape and kill anyone in the camp who might attempt a dash for freedom.

Desperate people seeking shelter at the camps quickly realized that there was no hope of ever leaving. Children born in the camps will marry and produce four to eight children of their own, and will likely die there. The refugee camp will become their life story, their history. They were stuck inside the camp. I saw the hopelessness in their faces and desperately prayed for their release from this forlorn life.

The camp set new standards for austere medicine, if it could even be called medicine. The doctor, more like a self taught EMT, did not have stethoscopes or blood pressure cuffs, no alcohol swabs, gloves or thermometers. Our pioneer barbers in the wild west had more medical equipment than these volunteers had.

The absence of electricity precluded any medical testing and all diagnoses were done by sight and touch. Even so, their skills were passed down through the generations and appeared adequate for treating common local ailments like malaria, dehydration, numerous intestinal parasites and frequent foot wounds.

Infant mortality was extremely high. I saw precious children with pus dripping from infected ears. In a few weeks their pain would go away, along with their ability to ever hear again – all due to the lack of inexpensive antibiotics. The tears that resulted from this realization added more stinging to my eyes, already on fire from the long, hot, sweaty day.

Medications were scarce, if not completely nonexistent. In their "pharmacy," the doc showed me four small packets of expired Cipro. There was an absence of ordinary items easily found in my own medicine cabinet at home: pain medications, aspirin, band-aids, Neosporin.

They were out of malaria drugs, so they brewed a local herb, artemisia, into a foul-tasting tea. I gagged down a cup and believed it killed everything in its gravitational path: all forms of cancer, TB, hepatitis A to E, yellow fever, and any other bonus ailment. I was sure that it must prevent dementia because I will never forget this remedy or this place.

Toilet facilities were plentiful and could be found just behind the nearest bush. They used bushes instead of toilets. I did not see a single square of toilet paper, a Sears catalog or any corn cobs conveniently stashed near these bush "latrines."

There was the basic lack of sanitary conditions in the camp. There was no getting desensitized to the idea of drinking the polluted water, nor any way to develop immunity to it. The only way to get clean water was to boil it.

There was no adequate shelter when the monsoons came. During the torrential rains, every life event occurred in the polluted mud. When the monsoons left, the swarms of mosquitoes returned. It was beyond imagination. You sat, ate, slept or otherwise functioned in a muddy, filthy, germ and mosquito-infested environment.

For us, even during the daytime, mosquitoes felt like demonic pests siphoning off the 115º perspiration streaming down our faces, followed by the inevitable drilling into our skin sucking on our blood.

Accompanying the mosquitoes were flies that orbited our heads and made passes at our sweat-filled eyes. Magnificent moths were so big they should have been required to file flight plans.

There was a reason these desperate refugees were called "the Mud People." When food was absent, they would eat the polluted mud. I did not see any cats or dogs at the camp. Anything with four legs was treated as protein.

We were forced to depart before late afternoon because the rebels attacked cars during the darkness. But, I could not just walk away without someday returning with medicines, nets and toilet paper.

We discussed returning to Gorome. Our small group, led by Rev. Dr. Bill Rapier from African Leadership Development[24], would hand carry vital medicines that were paid for by generous donors.

We could not do everything for the residents of Gorome, but we determined to bring our specialty of training pastors and developing leaders to grow communities of faith and hope.

That night my sleep was restless. The peoples' faces scrolled through my mind and their stories chronicled the evil deeds of their demonic rulers. I could not help hating their government.

Yet, if I had the power to remove those currently in power, what system would replace them? If history repeats itself, most likely the next one would be worse.

When I returned from South Sudan, I described the place as terrifying, dangerous and very dark. Part of me did not want to go back, but we all believed that God had arranged Divine Appointments with top government leaders and clearly opened opportunities where we could make a difference.

Several friends sent letters with their donations in support of my mission and ministry, First Response Chaplains of California. One person wrote, "Toby, I have a really bad feeling about this. Don't go. Don't go. Don't go."

---

[24] For more information on this vital work: aldafrica.wordpress.com

If my little light shines in dark places, South Sudan should be dark enough. It is. However, going back felt like a death sentence.

I was conflicted, not wanting to go back into the extremely dangerous camps, but seeing the opportunities offered to us. I was confused. If the Lord wanted me there, why did I have the heart attack that destroyed any chances of returning with my team?

Postscript: Only a few weeks later, the fragile social order broke down and the slaughter resumed in South Sudan. Last night I stood outside my home and looked up at the stars. Over 8,000 miles away under the stars were pastor friends in South Sudan running for their lives and hiding in the bush.

Another ten thousand refugees would be slaughtered, including Rev. Daniel Giel Pal, former Moderator, Eastern Upper Nile Presbytery, who was killed by government forces in Malakal on January 21, 2014.

For decades I have the following statement in a small frame on my desk that describes reality:

Sometimes God allows the faithful to be overcome, overthrown, even killed by the unfaithful. That is certainly the hardest aspect of standing alone. Here, you have given your all. You have stayed with the faith. You have supported God. But you too go down with the ship. Being right does not always mean being victorious. Being faithful does not always mean being successful. Remember that when you stand alone.

Report 36   Listening To Our Mistakes

Some stories are so painful to write and this is one of them. Unlike all the other stories in this book, this one is fictional... sort of. The reason I say it is fictional is because I cannot disclose names, dates or places. In the absence of facts, I must call the following fictional - sort of.

The trip to the remote, isolated village was long, hot and dusty. Again, the road was jolting, scarred with potholes the size of trucks and able to swallow a full-grown man. My head bounced around like a bobble-head doll on the dashboard of a car.

However, we did not let that diminish our thankfulness at being permitted to be here in South Sudan. Nor did we let anything else lessen the exuberance and joy we felt at the thought of having this enormously helpful project to offer to these villagers who truly had nothing.

As we approached the first of two villages, we crossed a river and saw numerous crocodiles lounging on the shoreline. "Probably not a good place to swim," jested one of my partners. "How does a kid learn to swim?"

"That is why most Sudanese do not know how to swim," commented the other partner who has spent most of his adult life in Africa. "Too dangerous."

We crossed over the low bridge and about a hundred yards later, we pulled off the road next to the first of a hundred round huts. A woman wearing a colorful everyday dress came out to discover who the visitors were.

We introduced ourselves and asked to meet the tribal Elder. She asked us to wait while she trotted to the interior of the village to find their leader. Women in other huts stood at their doorways with children hitched to their hips.

A dozen children seemed to come out of nowhere and swarmed around us. We easily recognized them as orphans because they were unattached to a parent, wore tattered shirts, no shoes and had disheveled hair and a gaunt look. Two of them were curious and touched my white hands with their index fingers.

Seeing my smile and feeling safe, the two of them wrapped their skinny arms around my legs and sat on my shoes. I realized that they wanted to ride on my shoes and rocked to signal me to walk around. Decades ago, my son did the same thing and when my grandchildren were small, they too took the identical position. I wondered if this simple pleasure might be a universal delight for youngsters.

The two little boys had big, chocolate brown eyes made to appear larger and even more endearing because of the sizable white area surrounding their brown irises. Their wide smiles displayed their brilliant white teeth as they giggled with simple pleasure of riding on my feet.

I took a few steps and their gleeful squeals signaled their joy. My blue eyes and their brown eyes connected. Two other orphans put their arms around my waist and wanted to take their turn on my feet. Others just wanted to be picked up. The three of us partners became human playground equipment for the children.

They were so cute. I wished I could have taken them home and given them the love and care they needed. More than a decade ago, one of my partners, Bill Rapier, did adopt two South African babies who were born to mothers who with AIDS. The babies were also thought to have AIDS, but both turned out to be free of the virus and are now healthy teenagers.

The woman who initially greeted us escorted a lean older gentleman to us. He had a dignified bearing as he approached. Without knowing our purpose, he took the initiative to invite me to his hut a short distance away. My two partners continued to entertain the children by our Land Rover.

The Elder spoke fluent English and invited me to sit on a three-legged stool. He gestured to his wife to bring us tea. He introduced himself and his clan. Three of the women could have been wives, but that was not clear. Numerous children ran in and out of the round hut with a thatched roof.

My preferred style of negotiating is to jump to the bottom line and try to make a deal. We could be in and out in 20 to 30 minutes, I figured. Not in Sudan though. This meeting moved at a steady pace, more like glacier speed - lasting almost four hours, during which my two other friends and more tribal leaders joined us.

The Elders were quiet and dignified and served us generous amounts of tea. They were always respectful toward us, but appeared cautious with their words, carefully considering each one before releasing it. Sometimes a pause between sentences lasted a minute. We had to learn how to handle the long periods of silence.

We waited and sipped more tea. My bladder was so full I figured that it would get stretch marks. We were more than two hours into this conversation and had not brought up our purpose. At this pace we had at least another hour to go. Instead, it turned out to be two more.

We sipped, waited, chatted and waited. I had to control my need to fill the dead air with words. I waited for a mysterious level of trust to be reached before we could bring up our purpose.

If we were to introduce our desire to build, staff and supply an orphanage prematurely, they would have dismissed us. Our trip would have been wasted.

"Who are you?" they asked before discussing any other subject. It was far more important to the Elders to know who we were... than what we wanted.

My partner has spent most of his life working with African pastors and knew that we should not disclose our purpose until the Elders felt like they knew us. Finally, after drinking at least a gallon of tea, the time was right.

"Do you have any orphaned children?" I asked casually. "Children without either parent?" We explained that when we drove up, we saw a dozen children who seemed to fall into this category.

The Elders looked at each other wondering if the other knew the answer to our question.

"I do not know," one finally said. "Come back tomorrow and I will tell you."

We were surprised by his response. How could he not see the same children who clung to our legs and laughed delightedly?

The thought of repeating that torturous trip with the enormous potholes seemed overwhelming. We honored his request and told him we would return the following day.

With a few more hours of daylight left, we went to a second village and got the same response: Come back tomorrow. While there, we spotted at least eight children who fit our profile of orphans.

The thought of repeating this trip the next day meant we would suffer more self-inflicting injuries. That night, back at our safe-house, I took a fist full of Tylenol for what felt like whiplash.

Note to self: Next time, bring a neck brace.

The following day we returned to meet with the first tribal Elder. He greeted us warmly and invited us into his home. We asked if he had found any orphans and anticipated him welcoming our offer of an orphanage. We waited for his reply.

"There are no orphans." We were puzzled when he declared it as a matter of fact.

Indeed, we did not see any orphans on this return trip. Why not? Were we missing something? I wondered if perhaps his response had something to do with his culture or language. There was not enough information for me to process his response.

We hurried to the second village nearby. That village Elder told us the very same thing as the Elder in the first Tribe.

"There are no orphans." Again, we were confused.

Back at the safe house, I took a more robust pill to deal with the pain of today's challenging drive.

The three of us dined that evening at a table with a woman who was a children's researcher with UNICEF for the United Nations. The protocol for getting acquainted with a new dinner guest was to describe our current mission and exchanging bits of personal information.

Eventually, the conversation turned to our mission of setting up orphanages in other countries and our hope to do the same in the villages we had just visited. We explained briefly how grateful we were to have received the go-ahead from the national political leadership, the funding from generous donors and the people willing to donate the labor and supplies to bring the project to life.

She listened very carefully as we shared that the tribal Elders in both villages reported, "There are no orphans," even though we saw about a dozen at one village and another eight the day before and that they were hanging on our legs and wanting to be picked up and held.

"Oh, my God!" the children's researcher with UNICEF gasped. "Please tell me you did not!" We nodded, but I got the sinking feeling that she was going to give us terrible news. She dropped her head and sighed, obviously searching to find words to explain the mistake or blunder we made, what she knew and we did not.

"We don't 'officially' know what happens to those children." She disclosed that in the past, others had the same humanitarian intentions, met with tribal Elders and received the same response.

I was excited to learn whatever mistakes we made so as to not repeat them. If the three of us had not had that chance meeting with this kind stranger from the UN, we never would have had any sort of understanding.

She said, "The children just disappear."

"Disappear?" I asked with a puzzled look. "Are they sent out of sight of our prying, meddling Western ways?" I speculated. "Are they hidden in the surrounding bush?" I was hopeful that she would have some answer.

"The Elders" she spoke slowly, "interpreted your offer of an orphanage as an attempt by the government to change their way of life."

She continued by explaining that despite our charitable offer, introducing an orphanage would impose unwanted change; that the Tribal Chief could not risk jeopardizing their way of life by allowing outsiders among them.

"The Tribal Chief has found that the only way they know how to thwart this is to remove the orphans from your curious eyes." There was a long pause.

"Their solution is to throw the orphans in the river to the crocodiles."

My mind flashed to the memory of the nearby river and the prehistoric beasts, the crocodiles we had seen the day before. The synapses in my brain short-circuited and I dissociated for a minute.

"Their solution...?" I thought! Killing children is not a solution. My mind tried to grasp what she said by internally repeating her statement. "Their solution is to throw the orphans in the river to the crocodiles."

I imagined that after our visit, men of the village were tasked that night with gathering up the orphans. An adult male could easily restrain a child like the ones who were sitting on our shoes. Those orphans wanted me to hold them in my arms, but now were carried by other men... to the river... to a horrible death.

At first the children would not know what was happening, but as they approached the river, the sight of the crocodiles had to have struck panic in their innocent souls. Their joyful, trusting eyes dashed about in fright as they took in the ghastly sight before them.

At the water's edge, the disposal process would be done quickly and probably done by two men – one man held the two little hands and the other held the child's feet. Then would begin a swing to launch them into the swirling waters where 500-pound beasts with sharp teeth and gaping jaws waited.

The joyous squeals earlier that day would have turned into terrified screams as the waiting children watch another child being flung into the night air and land in the water. Two or three crocodiles would lunge toward a helpless child and fight over the Tribe's Final Solution by chomping their powerful jaws over a part of the small body, crushing their bones.

The crocodile's huge tail would thrash violently and flip its body over to drown its victim. They would swim away to swallow a body part. Then more hungry crocodiles would move into the position where the next terrified orphan would be thrown.

Finally, the water would be silent. All the orphans were gone. The Tribal Chief could honestly tell us, "There are no orphans."

Meanwhile the UNICEF researcher continued speaking, but I could understand anything she said until the shock of this horrendous reality somewhat lessened. When my mind was able to engage back into the conversation, I felt sick to my stomach. One of our team members stepped outside and repeatedly vomited onto the flowerbed.

"Why didn't they just tell us they were not interested in our help?" I asked.

"In their culture, that would be impolite," she said as a matter of fact. "You need to understand; that village has survived a thousand years by not allowing change. The Elder knows that if he let you into the village, you would bring change... and for the village to survive, he cannot allow you to help."

When reviewing this tragedy with a missionary from the Congo, she observed, "The Tribe was probably looking for an excuse to get rid of these orphans anyway. They barely have enough to feed their own children. To feed the orphans meant families had to take food from their own children." Her reasoning was utilitarian but made sense. "Besides, this terrible act was more merciful than dying of starvation which is a far more cruel way to die."

It became crystal clear to us that in the future, we would have to find a different way to help the orphans without causing the Elders to kill them.

We could never again let the best of our intentions be our only guide. We need accurate information on each area we plan to visit.

Remember: This written account was pure fiction... sort of. I still have nightmares and find it difficult to get over my guilt. As I said at the beginning of this Report, some stories are just too painful to write and definitely, this is the worst.

Report 37   Listening for Solutions

"So, how do we set up systems to care for the orphans?" I pondered on my flight back to Juba, the capitol of South Sudan. I took my assigned seat next to a handsome South Sudanese man who began a friendly conversation as soon as I fastened my seatbelt. It turned out that Pastor James Tor was also a Presbyterian minister who ran an orphanage in his village.

For me, this was a clear Divine Appointment, as if God used the ticket agent to place us together. He shared his story with me, giving me deep insight into not only his personal life, but also into the daily struggles and suffering of those in his country of South Sudan.

Tor was kidnapped by rebels when he was twelve years old. Some of the children who were stolen were forced to become sex slaves until age fourteen when they were put into the military. When he was first kidnapped, Tor was trained to use an AK-47 and "at 19 I joined the fight." He was sent into combat, "a child soldier in an adult war."

In one horrific battle with other rebels, he and several other boy soldiers were wounded. Instead of receiving treatment for their wounds, his Warlord made a simple economic calculation: it was cheaper to replace a wounded soldier by kidnapping a new recruit.

"The other wounded boys and I were loaded into a pickup truck and taken to the river. Adult soldiers tossed us into the river with the crocodiles." For the crocodiles, it was feeding time; for the boys, it was a horrific end to a hopeless life.

In the gnashing, chomping, tail-slapping feeding frenzy, Tor escaped death by swimming to the other side of the river. "I was the only one who knew how to swim. None of my friends survived."

Tor recounted his grisly story smoothly and calmly, as though he had repeated it enough times to be able share it without reliving the trauma that it was. After wandering the streets, a Christian couple took him in and treated his wounds. They helped him with his education and he got involved with a local church.

"As you look back on your life, how do you relate to it now as an adult?" I asked.

"We fought like soldiers and died like children," Pastor Tor said quietly and looked down.

"Where was the church in all of this?" I was surprised by his answer. He turned his face to me and spoke so I could not miss his point.

"The church did not leave us; the pastors protected their people. They were stronger than the rebels' bullets, so the government kicked out the missionaries. Those missionaries were heroes. If not for the church, we would not have won the war to become the independent nation of South Sudan. Now we are free. Our children will hear how you American Presbyterians stood by us. Our grandchildren will hear how you did not leave us."

Reverend Tor eventually went to seminary and then started a church and an orphanage in South Sudan, Child Hope Restoration Mission (CHORM) located in Malakal to "help children escape the child soldier life and treat them for trauma, like Post Traumatic Stress Disorder (PTSD) issues."[25]

I believe that the population of South Sudan suffers from PTSD. For over a generation, they fought in an armed civil war among themselves and with the Islamic Republic of Sudan to the north. Estimates are that 2.5 million citizens were slaughtered; and the killing continues.[26] Because Pastor Tor had already set up an orphanage, I told him about our disastrous visits to the two villages and asked his advice on starting an orphanage.

---

25 American Psychiatric Association (2013). Diagnostic and Statistical Manual of Mental Disorders (5th ed.). Arlington, VA: American Psychiatric Publishing. pp. 271–280.

26 http://en.wikipedia.org/wiki/South_sudan

"To start an orphanage," Tor advised, "make it a joint effort with the local people, those who can take ownership of it. You will be a resource for training and give guidance in the background. They will know how to set up and run an orphanage." Our team's mistake was in trying to run it ourselves so as to not cause it to become a burden on them.

I have often wondered how people handle the pain of killing others. In another divine connection, I sat down under a large tree with a Christian leader, James, and learned that he also spent his teenage years as a rebel soldier in South Sudan. As he recounted his story, he spoke candidly about killing numerous enemy soldiers.

"How do you handle the pain?" I asked. He had a puzzled look and tilted his head as if he did not understand my question. "When you killed someone," I asked, "did you feel anything?" He shook his head, no.

"In America you can play war games on a computer, right?" asked James. I nodded; I had played them on an iPad and my grandchildren appear to me to be experts.

James inquired, "Did you feel any pain?"

"Of course not," I said, "It was just a game."

Yet, for James and his fellow-boy soldiers, they felt no difference between killing on a video screen and killing in real life. James felt nothing; he was numb. He seemed willing to speak about the subject, so I probed deeper.

"Did you ever have nightmares or subsequently feel any pain from the killing?" I asked. "Yes. Only once," he paused as a memory returned.

"I saw government soldiers kill my parents. Then, they stole our two chickens." I just shook my head slowly. "That was the last time I cried," he said in answer to my question about his pain.

"How did you work through your grief?" I asked.

"Grief became anger." James spoke in fragmented sentences. His answers dropped ordinary pronouns like I or me. By dropping the subject of the sentence, grammatically and psychologically, he was removing himself, dissociating from the events. "… joined the rebels and started killing," he said. I did not say anything. I just let him talk. "Killing often… many," he said in whispered tones. I wanted to ask how many, but I restrained myself.

James' life-story is not unusual among the Sudanese that I have been privileged to meet. There is unknowable, deep suffering that binds many in a common ministry of reaching out to those who know suffering for themselves. Both Tor and James engage others in experiencing mercy, forgiveness, healing, restoration and joy.

Report 38   The Power of Encouragement

After six hours, I wished I had never volunteered for this particular assignment. We did not know how steep and rugged the trail would be nor how the blazing sun would sear our unsuspecting bodies. We assembled a Strike Team, a group of five to seven personnel: two or three medical members, two armed guards, the Commo Guy (communications) and one Chaplain.

Here we were again, gasping in awe at the appalling, never-ending scenes of destruction, wounds and trauma before us. We treated a number of medical cases along the way up the trail: cuts, sprained ankles, diarrhea while the sun quietly beat the daylights out of us.

My first job on any deployment is to support all of my teammates, starting with the one nearest to me. By the end of the afternoon, I know their spirits are flagging and their bodies are worn down. The best thing I can do is give words of affirmation and encouragement. We all need to hear authentic and sincere statements of respect that can give strength to our souls.

As a Disaster Pastor and Chaplain on my medical team, I am a visible, physical, approachable symbol of comfort and help. I want to counsel, comfort and console. People may not be able to hear me above their inconsolable sorrow. I long to show the spiritual gift of mercy, for then I would be a tear-catcher, empathizing and feeling their pain with no need for words.

Each person wants to know that they are making a difference and are a vital part of the team. When I catch someone sacrificially working or performing a heroic act, I brag to the rest of the team. "Hey, you should have seen Mark handle that patient. He was brilliant!" By the end of the deployment, I will have praised every single team member... all of them are that good!

I have seen this team stitch up bullet holes while standing in sewage. Saturated in toxins, they delivered babies while using flashlights. Without electricity or ventilators, exhausted team members bagged breath into the lungs of the near-dead.

While working among the dead, team members brought the wounded back to life. On one occasion, they triaged over 800 patients before being forced to flee. Though ill-equipped, understaffed, exhausted, contaminated and isolated, this team helped pull-off the largest medical evacuation in history.

My team's purpose and my prayer as their Chaplain, is to "comfort the suffering, heal the broken, give hope to the broken-hearted, to shine light into the dark places of despair and to bring the ministry of heaven to hell."[27]

While I may whine and complain in my journal, I never share it with a teammate. If someone shares a complaint with me, I will acknowledge their statement by saying something like, "I hear 'ya."

If I am suffering from the heat, I know the sun is grinding on them too. Mosquitoes are biting all of us and everyone's muscles and joints are burning just like mine. For me to complain would only add a greater burden to those teammates who are also giving out of their reserves of energy, skill, knowledge and generosity.

This day, after hiking that rugged trail, we came to a rubble field where a barefoot teenage girl hobbled over to our strike team with a severe limp. One of our nurses knelt down beside her wounded left foot.

Even to my untrained eye, I surmised that the girl must have stepped on something several days earlier for the wound to be as ghastly as it appeared. The infection had spread well beyond the initial injury site. It looked nasty.

A medic from our team squatted down to join the nurse and they discussed the best course of action for this girl's treatment. I stood nearby, listening to their conversation and prayed silently.

---

[27] Unpublished manuscript, Toby Nelson, *Survival at the Superdome*, p.1.

The girl spoke no English, but with hand motions the nurse signaled her to lie down on her back in the dirt - in the dirt with no grassy area, no blanket to spread, no pallet, and certainly no bed or anything resembling what we might find in standard medical treatment areas in America.

"This looks really bad," the nurse commented to the medic while keeping a pleasant, undisturbed expression on his face. The girl did not understand our words, but she was watching their faces intently to get a read on what was happening.

With the same calm expression, smiling at the terrified teenager, our nurse asked the medic, "Has it gone septic?" He was questioning whether or not the infection had entered the blood stream. This often leads to shock, organ failure and ultimately, death.

A sepsis diagnosis normally calls for a very fast trip to an emergency room and the immediate administering of antibiotics and fluids. That is what it would mean in America, but we were kneeling on a dirt path with locals milling around us, a goat grazing a few feet away, with dust and flies everywhere.

The medic felt her forehead for evidence of fever, wrapped the blood pressure cuff around her slender arm, pumped the bulb to inflate the cuff and watched as the meter descended through the numbers. Sepsis presents symptoms of high fever and low blood pressure, and we were all surprised when he reported, "For now she's normal!" The medic was surprised too.

The nurse reached into his backpack and pulled out a few gauze pads, a scalpel and a bottle of water.

"How do you want to treat this?" the medic asked the nurse warily. I could tell from her tone and body language that she was aghast at the prospect of what would soon become this girl's treatment.

The teenaged girl was still closely observing their faces and began to visibly stiffen at any change in tone or expression. She did not know what they were planning, but it was evident that fear had begun to creep into her countenance.

"Let's start cleaning out the wound and see what we find," our nurse answered calmly. "Our options are so limited."

As the RN began to cut away the dead infected flesh, the girl released a primal scream with flailing arms as her body writhed. They told me to restrain her arms so that they could attend to her.

I moved in closer, eye to eye with the distressed patient, hearing her piercing, high-pitched cries. I could see and smell this deep infection.

Despite the surrounding drama, I was distracted by a horse fly that boldly sucked on the perspiration dripping off my eyelid.

I could not brush it away without releasing one of her arms, so I had to ignore it and everything else that would distract me.

Her eyes were panicked, as they glared into mine. Even without understanding her words, I knew she was saying. "What are you doing to me? Stop hurting me!" Lying flat on the ground, she could not see what our medics were doing at the other end of her body, but she must have been wondering if they were trying to cut off her foot. That decision would come soon enough.

"You are safe and you are going to be okay," I calmly said in English, trying to smile with my eyes. Of course, she did not know what I was saying and I am certain she did not care. All she knew was that she was in excruciating pain and a guy who looked like a priest and spoke a foreign language was forcibly restraining her.

When the girl sought our help, unaware of what would transpire, I am sure she did not anticipate this extreme level of pain. She was probably wishing they had just smeared some ashes and manure on her wound or that she had taken her chances with basic tribal doctoring.

We had nothing to relieve her pain, not even an aspirin. All we had were instruments that intensified her suffering. Unfortunately, we could not explain anything to her. The medic and nurse worked as quickly as they could; but for this girl, it was not nearly fast enough.

In the brief moments between her distressful wailings, I caught snippets of conversation from my teammates starting with:

RN: " ... whole foot looks infected."

Medic: "... amputation?"

RN: "Probably... but not here... bandage her up for now."

All the while, locals were drawn by the girl's screams and were pressing closer to see what was causing the distress. Our guards stepped up, motioning to the gathering crowds to keep their distance or continue moving along the trail.

The RN and the Medic had a brief discussion about whether to carry her back to our clinic or medevac her via helicopter to a hospital ship anchored in the bay.   However, we had no stretcher and even if we had one, the thought of carrying this screaming, writhing girl over rough terrain sounded torturous and inhumane.

"Our clinic will close in a few minutes," said one of our nearby team members. The nurse decided to finish wrapping the wound and then sent the girl away with instructions to come to our clinic the next morning. No one argued.

I wished this girl could have understood English so that I could have comforted her. I hoped that at least she had read in my face and body language that we were trying to bring healing to her.

I wish I could forget these experiences. I have seen more dead bodies than I can remember and held the dying in my lap. I have tried to compartmentalize the accumulated horrors and stuff them into a distant subconscious lock box. In the darkness they fed off each other and their corrosive powers leaked out.

I have seen what humans were not wired to look at. I have witnessed what should not have happened; I have been present as the unthinkable materialized. I have watched the unimaginable take shape, the forbidden become permissible and the offensive become a regular practice. I have seen nightmares come to life. I cannot "un-see" these images that are branded into my memory. All of the past experiences shape my present.

The Human Cry in me shouts, "Lord, help me!" And with that admission of inadequacy and pain, somehow grace appears. I ask the Lord to put the tormenting thoughts aside until it is time to begin my recovery back home.

Report 39   Choosing Between Wrong and Wrong

On one particularly grim mission, my team and I were working frantically to assess and transport as many critical, but salvageable, patients as possible. The only resource we had to transport our sick, wounded and injured was a squadron of Blackhawk helicopters and their heroic crews who had just returned from combat missions in Iraq.

Equipped as gunships and troop carriers, and definitely not fitted for medical transport, they landed and took off every two minutes so they could quickly evacuate our special-needs patients to some distant hospital.

Using Blackhawks fresh from combat missions was not ideal, but it was what we had and we were extremely grateful for them. Bear in mind, these same crew-members had been handling machine guns just a few weeks earlier. When they were deployed to this mission of mercy, crews first had to remove the .50 caliber machine guns mounted in the doors.

In hindsight, they probably should have left the guns on board, because our medical team later ended up needing protection in order to escape from gunfire in the area. Lawless locals were perched like snipers on top of buildings and intermittently both shot at the helicopters and at us as we loaded patients.

A paramedic team member who had accompanied a flight of injured and wounded people heard bullets fly through the cabin of his rescue helicopter. Tink! Tink! Tink! What an awful irony it would have been if the flight crew managed to survive Iraq, only to die in a civilian rescue mission.

As a result of the gunfire, the landing zone was eventually closed and the lifesaving flights terminated. In spite of this danger, a few hours later, one very brave crew risked their lives to pick up a final load of patients.

We had to make the difficult decision of selecting which patients would be the last to be rescued by helicopter. It was as if no matter which patients were chosen, the selection process itself felt bad, incredibly bad, and each choice would haunt me even years later.

One question is always present: On what basis should the medical team decide which patients should be put on rescue helicopters when everyone deserves to live? In ideal times, everyone is equal in worth so the most needy go out first. In a disaster, the needs of the individual are outweighed by the needs of the community.

For example, a newborn might live 80 years versus an 80-year old might only live another year. It was not that one life was more important than another; it was that rescuing infants increased the probability of our saving the maximum number of lives and lifespans.

The physical fact that so many tiny babies could be loaded into the same space that one adult would occupy was instrumental in the decision we ultimately made.

We concentrated on rescuing the infants who had so much life before them. It was gut wrenching determining the values of lives, but that is the nature of triaging mass casualties.

We all have equal worth in God's eyes, but for me, this, my first involvement in massive triage, I felt as if I had usurped part of God's role in determining who lives and who dies. Even our long-time surgeons were grieved at having to make these forced choices.

Every decision felt like a choice between wrong and wrong.

We decided to send the rest of the newborn babies, the most helpless and vulnerable, out on the last flight. Those babies needed rehydration and immediate medical attention to continue to live, neither of which we could adequately provide. There was a shortage of everything on site, especially basic supplies a newborn would need like water, formula, and diapers.

Newly born babies and toddlers of every imaginable condition, and some unimaginable ones, were hustled to us for transport. The extremely sick ones made no sounds at all. But, the healthy newborns squalled for attention and food, although there was none to be had.

The pitifully crying newborns pierced our outwardly calm façades, but they were not as disturbing as the tiny, silent ones. However, these tiniest babies had a more hopeful future than some of the critically ill or injured adult patients.

After the initial triage decisions were made, the next issue that fell upon us was to determine whether or not to send a baby with her family of three plus, or to use all the space in the medevac for only babies.

"Please, God, speak to us!" I prayed. The Voice was silent. When the Voice is silent, I have learned that often I am going through a learning curve. For guidance, I return to the most recent lesson that God is teaching me.

It was reminiscent of the times when my school teacher would verbally present lessons and then remain silent when she gave us a test. It felt the same with God; sometimes the Voice is present and sometimes there is silence.

Our team leaders instructed us to wrap each baby in a towel for the flight. These babies had in effect become bio-hazards as a result of the wretched conditions during their births. In our makeshift Delivery Room, they were born, handed to Mom, the cord was snipped, then the afterbirth dropped to the filthy floor, which was already deep in sewage.

There were simply no supplies or extra hands to welcome them properly. Some still wore the vernix of newborns, that waxy covering that would normally be bathed away in the nursery. The idea of sending unidentified babies (no wrist band, no birth certificate) swaddled in soiled towels with no clothing, to a distant host city and with no means of reconnecting them to relatives was so repugnant, we did not dare dwell on it.

We carried newborns in our arms to a landing zone a hundred yards from our medical aid station. As we handed each precious towel-wrapped baby to the crew chief of the flight, I wondered if their hysterical mothers would ever be able to find them.

"Where are you taking my baby?" screamed mothers. We had no way of knowing which specific hospital the helicopter would take the babies.

"Ma'am, I don't know," I confessed. "I'm so sorry." What I never told them was that in the absence of any identifying wristbands, documents or markings on their tiny bellies, in my mind, the chances of a reunion in the immediate future did not seem very good at all.

How long after a baby is born does a mother still recognize its cry and the shape of its face? Would she recognize her baby from the dozens of others?

Had we done this a week earlier before the disaster, it would have been scandalous, even criminal. However, the only way we could save these tiny lives was to evacuate them, separating them from their families.

The thought of what we were doing was unconscionable. We shoved it to the back of our minds, insensibly hoping its memory might mercifully fade. Normally, we would have kept families intact, but "normal" was long gone at this disaster and it was live or die for these helpless tiny newborns.

I returned home from that disaster mission after spending most of the flight crying silently. I walked through the front door around 3:00 a.m. The house was quiet, the family asleep. I set my long bag and backpack on the floor by the front door.

Before heading to my bedroom, I wanted to check on our three-month old grandson. Our son, his wife, their son, Judy and I were living together at the time while I pastored a church in the San Francisco Bay Area.

After working and sleeping on contaminated floors for the past few weeks, walking on carpet felt strange – opulent. I quietly approached our grandson's crib and in the dark saw him in little white sleepers, comfortably sprawled on a clean baby blanket. His face was cherubic and I marveled at his beauty and the potential of his future.

Then, mental whiplash rocked my brain.

Only a few hours earlier, a desperate mother with outstretched arms had handed me her baby who was about the same age as my grandson. I picked up our little baby, cradling his head and neck with my left hand and placing my right hand under a loaded, mushy diaper. The diaper oozed its contents onto my hand and wrist, but I was well past being squeamish, because in my most recent world, everyone and everything was contaminated.

Holding my precious grandson, Sam, I mentally flashed back to the disaster. In my memory, a mother was shouting something at me, her voice blending with other human cries and the roar of the nearby Blackhawk. I tried to read her lips as she was apparently yelling out a name. But because of the growl of the aircraft, all I heard was something that sounded like a sneeze.

"Okay," I shouted back. "We'll take care of her!"

"He's a boy!" she shouted back.

I handed the baby to the nurse. She ripped off the contaminated diaper and let it fall to the ground, where everything landed anyway. Yep, he was a boy. Holding him in one hand against her chest, she grabbed one of the contaminated towels and wrapped him in it. It was all we had.

The nurse handed the baby boy through the cabin door of the helicopter, into the beefy arms of a crewmember. With the baby safely in his arms, he backed into the cabin, shut the door and the Blackhawk lifted off for the last time.

I watched the helicopter take the tiny boy and the other babies over the horizon into the unknown.

"Lord, get these babies back to their mothers," I fervently prayed as I had for all the other babies.

After a few minutes, the flashback lifted and I mentally returned to the reality of my own flesh and blood, my baby grandson. My tears again fell, but these were tears of heartfelt gratitude for this precious new life I loved with all my heart and soul.

At the disaster, I had been overwhelmed with gratitude that all of our team members knew their jobs and gave every part of themselves to providing superb medical care. I also thought of our nurses deftly handling the soiled babies, the crewmembers working methodically to load and take off and the guards protecting all of us.

What a perfect blend of skills and talents God had brought together as we struggled through every difficult component and every heart-breaking moment of this disaster. Each time we are called to a disaster, we gather together to give our collective best, to offer what help we can. I praise God for each person on this gifted medical team that is tasked with making these difficult choices.

Walking to the changing table with my grandson in my arms, I thought how remarkable it was that the last baby-lift had been less than twenty-four hours ago. Then, returning my clean grandson back to his crib, my throat tightened at my incredible blessings.

Tears of gratitude were finally able to flow as my body shook convulsively with the profuse release of pent-up emotion. With this, I began my upcoming emotional journey of reconnecting with normal life.

Disaster missions do something strange in my head. While I am at a disaster, I know I will leave the area within a few weeks after my arrival. Somehow, my surroundings become my new normal and my mind quickly adjusts to the immediate chaos.

Counselors tell me that in disasters, I experience cognitive dissonance. I prefer my term - mental whiplash. What becomes normal at a disaster does not match the normal at home. And, whenever I return home, I feel disoriented. Off-balance.

One counselor pressed me to have more balance in my life. I know I should spread out my energy evenly between family, rest, nutrition, spiritual renewal, recreation and work.

I have two sober opinions: my counselor was right; there will never be balance in my life. Nor do I want it.

When I am with a disaster team the work is consuming, off the chart extreme. Nothing I do can be done half-heartedly or in moderation.

Half my brain stays hyper-vigilant; the second half feels vulnerable like I am dancing on a precipice, and the third half struggles to keep sane.

Before I went to bed, I stepped into the shower and another disconnect struck me. Here was water on demand, hot and clean! I scrubbed for half an hour, trying to wash away the contaminated memories. It takes time to fit back into normal routines. Coming home means coming down.

Report 40   The Why Question

The pace of activity on a deployment is so intense that there is little time for reflection on the bigger philosophical questions. These issues emerged one spring when I joined a disaster team that was faith-based.

We reported to the scene of a violent tornado in the South, where 64 lives were lost. The dollar amount assigned to this multi-city tornado was several billion... miniscule compared to the value of the lives lost.

I joined a small local group who was handing out MRE kits (Meals Ready to Eat) as quickly as we could release them out of the stacks of cases. It was vigorous work, non-stop and no breaks for food or restrooms. However, our efforts were nothing compared to what these folks had endured having lost everything but their lives.

As rapidly as we worked, the human line snaked slowly, like those zigzag lines at Disneyland. Food seemed tantalizingly close, but was still a few minutes away as the line wrapped around yet another roped barrier.

Standing close to us was a reporter who had his cameraman pan a population that had not yet been served. He announced, "These people are starving and have not eaten in days." He was almost correct, and yet misleading.

He told part of the truth, but he lied by omission, giving his audience the impression that all of the hungry survivors in this area would continue to go without sustenance, while a few feet out of camera range, hundreds were already tearing into the MREs.

"Why did you say that?" I challenged him. "We are serving the people as fast as possible and you did not convey the whole truth!"

"Well, Padre," he said confident and slightly condescending "that's your truth, it's not my truth. Besides, my producer wants to keep the crisis alive." Then he had his cameraman turn to me.

"So, Padre, how do you handle the chaos and death of a disaster?" I was still miffed, but thought that this might turn out to be an opportunity to bring out the whole truth.

"It's hard," I said. "There are lots of questions that I cannot answer." He pressed me for more. "I trust that God is still good, that God is still sovereign, that there is still a plan," I said. "God is going to help us, comfort us, heal us, and put our lives back together." There are mysteries I do not like, questions that refuse to be answered, especially during the immediacy of a disaster.

"Why did God allow this disaster to happen?" he prodded.

"The better question is, 'why aren't there more people here to help?'" I shot back.

We all have "why" questions that never get answered. Jesus learned this when he was on the Cross, crying out, 'Why, why, Father, have you forsaken me?'[28] Even he was not given an answer."

God seldom answers our "why?" questions. That really disturbs me. What I know is how to work in darkness. With even a little light there is no amount of darkness that can put out that light from God. But the "why?" question is different because God chooses to hide the answer in mystery.

"Was this disaster punishment from God?" the reporter pressed.

I answered that I would like to think not, but I did not know. There seems to be a disaster at one place or another in the world at any given time. Some of them are caused by our poor choices of earth management; others appear to be random.

We do not live in a world of peace that is interrupted by disasters. We live in a world of disasters that are interrupted by seasons of peace.

---

[28] Matthew 27.46

The reporter continued as if trying to trap me theologically. Then came THE question: why does an all-powerful God not stop disasters from happening? I did not want to attribute blame to either God or the Devil. I wondered if perhaps this current tornado was just a horrendous combination of meteorological forces, the perfect storm.

If so, he asked, "why did not God, who created the earth change the weather by altering the meteorological forces?" It was the big picture of death and destruction that he seemed to be skimming over in his search for a pin-pointed sound bite.

I tried to move him away from the unanswerable "why" questions so as to focus on the reality of this present disaster scene. For me, the obvious focus at this disaster scene was to provide needed resources and not focus on imponderable questions nor assign blame.

Each natural or man-made disaster needs to be examined, analyzed, described, understood and remembered, so that we can be better prepared for the next one. With this reporter, my focus in the moment was to convey the impact of these huge life-changers while trying to concentrate on helping the hungry people.

It is my fundamental belief that our Agencies need to be adequately funded, better prepared, to secure enough necessary equipment and send more thoroughly trained personnel. For surely other apocalyptic events will happen again, perhaps even in our own neighborhoods.

When disasters come, we will most likely cast blame on God and attempt to discover if God visited this upon us as punishment. God forbid that we should forget what we thought we learned and that we continue to choose to treat the earth with such abandon.

I am grateful when news reporters tell us what happened in real time, preferably with film. We need to know what is going on so that we can make a difference with donations and volunteering. To me, this is the crucial function of news on disasters – suggesting how we can respond!

Later, I asked two of my fellow first responders if disasters raised such theological questions in their experiences. Both agreed that yes, questions do surface, and yet, the questions are completely imponderable and reach no satisfying conclusion. They were right.

Then one of them asked, "What theologian do you disagree with them most?" I was surprised by his question and paused for several moments. A couple of other team members overheard his question and turned to hear my answer.

"Jesus," I said. He was taken aback.

"Huh?," His eyes opened wide with surprise and he invited me to unpack my answer.

"Jesus' thoughts are higher than my thoughts and his ways are higher than my ways," I began. "He tells me to love people who have hurt me. I want to get even. Then he expects me to forgive them. I find it easier to hold a grudge. He tells me to bless those who curse me. I am more inclined to curse back. He tells me to repent and die to selfishness."

"Yet, you follow him," he observed. "Why?"

"No one else is worthy to follow," I said. "He brings out the best in me, he heals my inner wounds, he gives me hope in bad situations and he redeems the broken parts in me. He gets me to love the unlovely and serve the ungrateful."

Report 41   Telling Our Stories

I use the term "Survivor Ethics" as an attempt to offer an explanation for the dreadful choices we all must make when working at disasters - when we are forced to think the unthinkable, do the un-doable and utter the unutterable. So, I put my thoughts and feelings into my journals.

First responders will often find themselves dealing with messy choices. They will make the best choice possible given their circumstances, yet feel uneasy about it later. "Did I make the right choice?" I was inspired by an analogy Jesus used to describe these situations.

When we have plenty of time and information to make informed decisions, I call this Daylight Ethics. Here is what he said,

> "Are there not twelve hours of daylight? A person who walks by daylight will not stumble, for he sees by this world's light. It is when he walks by night that he stumbles, for he has no light."[29]

Jesus' observation became a metaphor for me. Just as natural light is a reliable resource for guiding us through the day, the absence of light leaves us vulnerable to hazards. I

---

[29] John 11.9 NIV

eventually coined the term Midnight Ethics to describe the ethical paradigm that I, and many others, adopted to help us navigate through those dark times with inadequate tools, medicines, personnel, etc.

Daylight Ethics guide most of us 99% of the time. According to the Daylight Ethical paradigm, our lives will be blessed when we are faced with ethical dilemmas if we take the time to carefully consider all our options, and their consequences, and make the best, or "right," decision that benefits the most people possible.

Midnight Ethics guide us 1% of the time, on those occasions when we fall under temporary darkness and our freedom to choose the best ethic is taken away - when choices are limited to bad and worse; when time to consider all our options is reduced to seconds; and when the consequences of our decisions seem cruel in any other context except in pure survival mode.

Midnight Ethics help us when all of the possible choices are wrong according to conventional codes of conduct or to our own deeply held values. In emergencies, Daylight Ethics are often powerless to restore peace and justice to our communities. Midnight Ethics are principles we instinctively adopt to empower us to chart a course of action when lives and our way of life are threatened.[30]

I have developed presentations to try to explain Survivor Ethics in a series of invitational speeches to church congregations, first-responders, disaster coordination meetings and to my own counselors.

If people hear the concept of Survivor Ethics, the more they will have a mental and moral grid to make difficult choices when they are not free to make the best one, the right one. This can offer a sort of therapeutic encouragement to suffering souls who have PTSD issues after working in the field of disasters, thus enhancing their healing with a qualified therapist.

I had just finished one of these presentations at Westminster Presbyterian Church across the street from the California State Capitol. It was well attended and I was pleased with the audience's response. They seemed to "get it". I was hopeful that the message would continue on into the night inside of each of them as they quietly departed.

I had packed up all of my speech-related gear (white board, flip charts, hand-outs – I am nothing if not well prepared to drive my points home) and was almost out the door when an elderly gentleman approached me. He walked slowly toward

---

[30] *Midnight Ethics*, an unpublished manuscript, 2014, p. 10.

me, leaning on a cane and noticeably limping. I was curious as he called out, "Pastor Toby, wait, please."

"Can we talk?" he asked. "Tonight you spoke the truth about why we soldiers do not tell our stories when we return."

Hmm. He heard me. He got it, and was repeating my own message back to me. This was a good start.

"We soldiers do not talk because in combat we have practiced 'midnight ethics' or witnessed those situations that can lead to 'survivor ethics.'" He quoted me almost perfectly.

"True," I concurred. He repeated what I had just taught in my lecture, "You probably tried to tell your stories a couple of times, but your friends and family reacted poorly, did not understand or perhaps did not want to understand."

"I tried to tell my stories... but folks did not want to hear them. At least now, because of your presentation, I know why."

I asked him, "How long have you kept your story inside?"

"Over sixty-five years," he replied.

"Is your story sixty-five years old," I asked gently, "or is it still fresh?"

"I relive the stories every day," he whispered, his voice choking. "What can I do?"

"You can still tell your story." I replied. "Your pastor was here tonight. Meet with him; tell him your story."

"Stories," he corrected me. "Stories!" he repeated with a little stronger voice.

Just then, the church custodian turned off the lights, not realizing we were still in the room. We stood there in the dark just two feet apart, but mysteriously in two different worlds. I was in the present; he was somewhere in North Korea, sixty-five years earlier.

"Hey!" he cried out in panic, "Let us out of here!" The lights came back on and we walked down the short hallway.

I commented on his limp that I had noticed earlier. He stopped and with his cane, he tapped his right ankle. "Clink." It was a prosthetic leg. What a great opening for me!

"How did you lose your leg?" I asked. We passed through the exit door and stepped into the darkness of the vacant parking lot.

"I lost it on a night just like tonight," he said while raising the end of his cane and pointing to the stars in the cold night sky. "I was freezing on a hillside in a fire-fight from Hell."

"But tonight is different," I said.

"How so?" he asked.

"For the first time in sixty-five years, you just told the first of your stories," I said. While I love ministering at a disaster I live for these Divine Appointments.

Over the years, I have found that many combat veterans admit that they do not discuss their feelings with their own close military pals even those who were there with them. I learned an analogy from a friend of mine who is a Purple Heart veteran, and it sums up what I had not been able to verbalize.

I asked Dave one day what had happened to his right index finger, which was missing, and he told me the story of the day he was wounded in Viet Nam. I do not recall all of the details, but it involved an ambush, muddy ditches, buddies falling around him.

Wounded and laying in the mud he shouted to his buddy who ran over to him. Dave reached up to grab the hand of his buddy when an enemy bullet took his finger off. I asked him if he ever relived the event.

"It is like a movie playing in the back of my mind," Dave said slowly. "It is always running... but I am not always watching it."

I understood what he meant instantly and realized that scenes mentally recorded from terrible disasters were also playing nonstop in my own head. Thanks to Dave's explanation, I have to give myself permission to choose not to watch it rather than let it consume me.

Telling our stories helps to bleed off some of the energy of the memories. Telling stories do not just convey information, they have the power to transform a person's life.

Report 42   My Father's Voice

Among the choices that were not mine to make were who my parents would be and the time and place of my birth. I was born at Quantico, Virginia, into the U.S. Marine Corps to a father who served as a decorated combat pilot for his career. Most of my childhood memories are a blur because we moved so often.

By the time I was 18, we had moved across the country ten times and lived in 18 homes. My sister, Leslie, who is three years younger, named ten different schools we attended while growing up. I clearly remember a personal disaster my father suffered and the life-giving words he spoke into my life when recounting it to me.

My father was unpacking a box after one of our moves across country. I sat on the floor beside him and watched him sort through dozens of old black and white photos of relatives, places we had lived and our immediate family. The pictures had been bundled together by a rubber band that had dried out and broke when he handled them.

I thought at the time that the pictures should have been organized in an album with names and dates to jog our memories in the future. But as I sat with my father that day, it was not the time to organize them into albums.

There was never time. He shuffled the pictures together like a deck of cards, wrapped them with a new rubber band and returned them to the box or threw them away.

Then he pulled out an old envelope stuffed with large photos - about a dozen military photos of a crash site. Unlike the previous bundles, he took his time gazing at these pictures. The earlier photos evoked simple image of ordinary life… however, these larger pictures summoned deeper, more complex memories.

Looking over my father's broad shoulder, the black and white photos showed the wreckage of a fighter plane spread over a hillside in North Korea. He held in his hands the source of his on-going night terrors.

He lingered over several pictures that appeared to transport him back in time to a cold night when he was flying a close air support mission for a Marine patrol. From his aerial view, my father could see that this patrol was about to be ambushed by North Korean soldiers who lay in wait for a fight just 200 yards away.

He made several passes over both the American and the North Korean patrols. His radio had failed and he had no way to warn the Marines of their imminent danger.

 The increasingly poor visibility required him to leave. He should have. However, one of the unique features of the

Marine Corps is that pilots and ground soldiers train together. He knew these men. They were friends. He decided to chance one more pass.

He dropped his altitude dangerously low. It was a risk, but he did not want to abandon his fellow Marines. Suddenly, he entered a patch of fog and his plane impacted on the jagged rocky mountainside.

Despite blood streaming from his head and feeling a sharp pain in his neck, he crawled out through the broken windshield of his destroyed aircraft. He was surprised to be alive. However, the night was not over.

The sound of the crash caused both patrols to converge on him. Within minutes the North Koreans found his crash site... and the shooting began. He took cover on the opposite side of the wreckage with only a revolver, a .38 caliber pistol, to hold off a dozen attackers.

Anxious and scared, he quickly fired off all six bullets at the approaching enemy. He searched for extra bullets in a small pouch on his gun belt. His fingers found six more bullets and his trembling hand held them tight so as not to lose any.

This time he decided to shoot only five at the enemy. The last bullet he reserved for himself. He had been warned that when the enemy captured American pilots, they chose to torture and kill them.   He was not going to give them that choice.

Trying to make every shot count was made difficult by the blood streaming into his eyes.   The sharp pain in his neck made aiming difficult. Then he heard sounds coming from behind him.   He figured the enemy had out flanked him. Exposed, he was now without cover. He was surrounded.   He spun around and took aim.

Just like in the movies, the Marines he earlier tried to protect now came over the hill to save him. They quickly set up shooting positions around his downed fighter plane. The firefight was on. For several minutes bullets filled the night darkness in search of new victims.

Hunkered near the side of the fuselage, the medic on the Marine patrol laid him on the ground to check him for injuries. Seeing blood flowing from under his flight helmet, the medic packaged him on a makeshift stretcher.

Under the cover of darkness, the Marines slipped away. The enemy lost their prize. My father would spend the next six months recovering from broken neck bones on a hospital ship called Mercy.

He threw the photos in a trash pile, these pictures that triggered terrible demonic nightmares. Maybe he thought by throwing them away he could delete them from his memory like we now do so easily with unwanted computer files.

The next photo brought a smile to his face. The picture he held had nothing to do with the crash scene. His eyes lingered on the image and his mind flew to another time and place.

I asked him what he liked about it. I should have been silent. The photo triggered a powerful memory that captured him unlike the North Koreans could have. Still holding the photo, he was reliving a deeply charged trauma.

It took a few moments for him to collect his thoughts. He handed me the black and white photo. It looked like so many other war photos of refugees amid destruction.

He found his voice and told me a story. Toward the end of his recovery from his neck injury, he was relocated to a land-based hospital in South Korea. One afternoon, he ventured off the base on a path in a secure area. He was caught up with gratitude at surviving the crash and was thoroughly enjoying the beauty around him when he came upon an interesting sight, the edge of a large crater in the earth that he or a fellow pilot had made by dropping a 500-pound bomb.

Standing halfway down the side of the crater was a Korean mother and her three toddler boys. No husband was around. My father surmised the missing husband was dead. Dug into the wall of the bomb crater was a cave that the four of them used as shelter.

Still recovering from his injuries, he carefully climbed down to the epicenter of the bombsite and framed the following scene in the viewfinder of his Rolleiflex camera.

Their home, a cave. The hand of the third boy is at the extreme right

"When I clicked the shutter button to take this picture," he said. "I made a choice."

"What choice?" I asked. The photo was interesting but it did not have any meaning to me.

"I saw what I was doing as a fighter pilot. I never felt good about the shooting and killing, the dog-fights, the strafing and the bombings, even though they were the enemy." This was a conflicted side to my father I had never known.

"But the war was on, I was a Marine Corps pilot and had a job to do." He was trying to explain something he still did not fully understand himself. "I just could not keep destroying things and killing people," he blurted out. My father was making a confession. "I just could not do it anymore." He felt a very dark stirring inside and needed to get a heavy burden off his chest … off his conscience.

"So, what did you do?" I asked.

"I switched from being a fighter pilot to rescue helicopters," he answered.

"Is that the reason you took up flying rescue missions?" I asked with surprise. I was always puzzled why he gave up the status of being a hotshot jet fighter pilot for flying a slow ugly MASH helicopter with a big red cross target on the side. We both sat silently.

Wherever that photo transported him, I wanted to know. It took a few moments for him to collect his thoughts.

His eyes focused on me and he was present. Rather than saying more about the picture, he used his role as a father to provide a teachable moment for me. A teachable moment is when a person is open to receiving an important life lesson from a mentor. When a good father speaks into the heart of his child, there is more than just the transfer of information.

Using only his words, his voice planted the seed of a deeply held, non-negotiable value that shaped the rest of my life. To do so, he explained how God used that plane crash and the photo, a personal disaster, to get him to make a hard choice: the choice to keep on killing as a fighter pilot or to do something more redemptive, become a rescue helicopter pilot.

"Son," now very present, "given enough time you will have to make choices for the sake of your conscience that will change the rest of your life." I felt uncomfortable not knowing what that might mean for me. Did he know something I did not? It would take time to find out.

"So that is why you chose to fly rescue helicopters?" I repeated awkwardly. He nodded. His voice was now too choked with emotion to speak. I did not ask for more. I inherited the same gag reflex when incredibly deep emotions try to surface. Our conversation was over. As a way to remember this moment he gave me the above black and white photo.

There was no way he could know my future. Without knowing what life changing choices I would eventually make, his voice was recorded in my heart: "Given enough time... you will have to make choices...."

The stories and teaching that my father gave me illustrated the core values that he himself had modeled and instilled inside of me.

It all led me to minister at the Family Assistance Center and Ground Zero after 9/11 and to make the life-choice of becoming a Disaster Chaplain, the Padre, on a Federal Disaster Medical Assistance Team. As this role broadened to joining and creating other disaster teams, people began to call me the "Disaster Pastor."

Report 43   Honest To God

The stories I have reported define who I am today. I acknowledge being trained, encouraged and hardened by my Marine Corp father, tenderized by the Spirit of God, directed by the Voice, supported by friends and loved by my family.

However, after years of serving as a Disaster Pastor and Law Enforcement Chaplain, I realized that I had been deeply affected by the fears, errors and horrors of this calling. I knew from having to live with myself that I had not even touched the top of my depths that seemed more like an abyss of pain... pain from serving as a disaster pastor.

It took decades to finally hear my own Human Cry. That Cry was a buried, compressed reservoir of pain, anger and guilt for my felt inadequacies and an overwhelming sorrow that I could not shake. Accessing the deepest part of my soul would take more skills than I internally possessed. I needed outside help.

Normally, I did what any pastor would do after returning from disaster relief assignments. I engaged in a few months of intense counseling, focusing on whatever might restore me to my old pre-disaster self.

However, after several more deployments, which internally felt like dozens, and subsequent counseling, nothing seemed to bring freedom from deeper issues that stubbornly remained hidden. Had traditional counseling just quit working for me?

Then, my rubber band of resiliency gave out and I snapped. I felt like a Humpty Dumpty pastor, beyond repair. Yet, as an introvert, all of this pain and confusion remained trapped inside.

To others, I seemed like the same old Toby, always ready with a smile and some humor. I was not purposely trying to ignore the pain or put on a façade of pretense.

We humans seem to carry around invisible giant trash bags stuffed with our emotional junk until there is no more room. Then the seam splits. It all starts spilling out, usually at the most inappropriate and embarrassing times. I desperately yearned to dump my built-up internal garbage, but did not know how.

The distress in my soul led to questions that seemed to defy answers. Unfortunately, no one else that I knew seemed to be asking the same questions.

I felt isolated, even though I was deeply connected to people who truly loved me. No amount of prayer could bring comfort to my deepest inner life, even as I proclaimed the truth of God's peace and power from my pulpit each Sunday - because it is the truth. What I did not know then was that God's plan for my healing would be a new, deeper work in my life.

My search for answers was hindered by the fact that I did not feel comfortable sharing details of what I had experienced while serving in roles as Senior Chaplain for First Response Chaplains of California, the Chairperson of African Leadership Development - a mission board focused on mentoring African pastors[31] and as a Presbyterian minister.

I instinctively presumed that unless someone had experienced what I had seen, heard and done during disasters, that person would not easily understand what I was experiencing as aftershocks. I was like the alcoholic who needed to talk to a recovering alcoholic. I needed to talk to a human and hear the voice of someone wise and safe, someone with insight into these intense life experiences.

With great caution, I sought the counsel of a dear friend, Dr. Robert Evans. He and I were senior pastors of two large neighboring churches in a suburb of San Francisco, California. Over time, we became trusted friends. I dared to hope that Dr. Evans, a man whose life was devoted to understanding complex ethical issues, could help me process what I was feeling.

"Do you have any books on 'Survivor Ethics?'" I asked. At the time, this term was my best attempt to conceptualize the abominations my team and I had experienced and the ethical

---

[31] For more information go to www.aldafrica.org

decisions we made so as to survive and do our jobs.

"What do you mean by survivor ethics?" Robert asked. He knew I had served as a Disaster Pastor in multiple disasters. He was not just interested in hearing the stories; he cared about me and realized that I needed help handling my tormenting memories.

"Survivor Ethics... That is a term I coined," I began, "to describe the terrible decisions some of us have been forced to make under such horrific conditions. Unfortunately, the truth of what actually happened has largely been censored out of the public's awareness.

We made the best choices we could under appalling circumstances and we participated in events that violated our consciences and seemed to me to fly in the face of the societal norms of right and wrong. These choices contradicted deeply-rooted ethical practices I have upheld as a Presbyterian pastor for over the decades."

"To my knowledge, there has never been a book written on that subject," he answered. "In fact, Survivor Ethics is a contradiction in terms."

"How so?" I asked.

"Because an ethical decision requires reflection. Survivors do not have time to reflect on their choices," he explained.

"That's what happened," I simply said. "There was no time.

There was no way we could have prepared for the dire conditions and painful decisions we would be compelled to make."

"I carry a lot of what feels like dark knowledge," I continued.

"I cannot 'unsee' these things. I've tried to shake them, nothing works. It feels like a permanent tattoo on my soul and I do not know how to handle it," I explained.

I suddenly realized this was the core of my turmoil. The memories were a conflict of expectations and were causing my insides to feel dark. Always before, turmoil could swirl outside of me, but could not touch the customary joy I felt inside. Normally my soul felt like a fresh water spring. Before, the feeling of the absence of God's presence was only momentary. Now, it had evolved into a permanent aspect of my everyday life.

I subsequently found out that many of my teammates felt the same way. Knowing that fact helped me not feel so alone, but it still did not solve my own personal imperative of longing to be free of the guilt and shame I now personally carried.

I often see traumatized people who are unable to process their experiences on their own. Like me, these individuals may be caught in cycles of guilt and self-condemnation as their memories haunt them and their consciences condemn them.

Conversations with Robert gave me permission to explore my memories – memories that conflicted with what I thought God should have done - without me experiencing a fear of judgment. Telling him my stories provided life-giving relief.

However, I still felt abandoned by the Silent One, and the absence of God's presence left a void that physically hurt. The pain felt like an unrelenting grief as if I had lost a loved one. If this ache were to be permanent, then this was going to feel like a very long life.

Report 44   God, where are you?

Would I ever feel intimacy with God again?

During this long process, I feared to express my anger at God with anyone, and especially to God. Verbalizing anger at God felt blasphemous. This notion probably came from my military family of origin, where we were not permitted to discuss our own feelings about anything. I assumed that what was happening inside of me was my fault, my sin, a fatal character flaw. If it were not my fault, what was going on?

Years later, I met with a Psychologist, Dr. John Patterson. He had me try a visualization technique to help me get back together with Jesus. He asked me to relax, close my eyes, and imagine sitting in an idyllic place. I pictured myself in an imaginary sweet spot where I was safe.

I saw myself sitting at a familiar picnic bench under a large shade tree at a harbor marina in Ventura, California. Muscles in my shoulders unknotted, the buzz in my head quieted and my soul felt peaceful. It was the first time in months that all felt right with my world. I could have stayed there for hours, but the per minute fee precluded frittering away any time.

"OK," the counselor said, softly. "Now, picture Jesus walking slowly toward you."

In my mind's eye, Jesus entered the picture about thirty feet away. I recognized him immediately. In my Anglo-Saxon American mindset, he was a white, blue-eyed, European male in his early thirties wearing a Middle Eastern linen robe like we see in religious pictures.

I knew that this was an Anglo-Saxon, Western stereotype and totally inaccurate; still, that was who showed up in my mind. Jesus moved slowly toward me until he stopped about eight feet away. A mysterious anxiety suddenly rose inside me.

"Now, picture Jesus reaching his arms out to you," suggested the counselor.

I reacted immediately, "Don't come any closer!" I barked out. My physical body recoiled involuntarily in a near fetal position, as if to protect itself from a sudden danger.

"Stop! Don't you touch me!" I ordered Jesus. He stopped and did not say a word. I felt greatly conflicted. Here I was, a seasoned, tested, deeply committed Presbyterian pastor telling Jesus to keep his distance. There was no denying, however, that I was filled with seething anger toward him.

"Tell Jesus what you are feeling," prompted the counselor. In my mind I changed his instruction to, "Tell Jesus your reactions." I don't have many feelings, but reactions I've got. I think my emotional wiring is simple, having a limited emotional range that can be reduced to four basic feelings: hungry, tired, amorous and angry. That's it!

Most would consider only the last one to be a genuine feeling and would treat the first three as physical conditions. Not me. I would have only one emotion if the other three were eliminated. So not wanting to appear too emotionally disabled, I include the other three.

During this cosmic confrontation, I railed, "Jesus, I am furious at you," there was anger in me that gave power to my words. "How could you let so many innocent people die?" My question sounded more like an accusation and to me, my words sounded blasphemous. God could strike me dead with a lightening bolt and certainly had the right.

But it did not matter; I had had it with the Absent One. All the peaceful relaxation I had before the counselor dragged Jesus into the picture was gone. In my mind, Jesus just stood there, listening to my ranting.

"You sent me into these hellholes and then abandoned me. In your day, you raised people from the dead. I believed you could at least keep people alive... instead you let them die in my lap." Jesus just stood there and said nothing.

"You are eternal, but I expected you to be present with me. I preach about you doing miracles. Well, I could have used a few. You say you are everywhere, but where were you when I needed you?"

"No wonder you do not have many friends!" I muttered.

I am never so mad as when God makes me angry. Why did I get so angry? My moral gut shouted, "I have the expectation that you are sovereign - that you can stop bad things from happening to good people. You need to replace your guardian angels if they do not protect the innocent ones," I demanded.

"You need to take some responsibly for these disasters. Someone Big is to blame for these messes!" After all, even insurance companies intentionally blame God when they label some events "Acts of God."

My anger revealed an assumption, a misconception, about God I had been carrying. Specifically, I expected that if God were the biggest power then God was responsible for this chaos and thus was accountable.

In fact, God does take credit for some disasters: "I form the light and create darkness, I bring prosperity and create disaster; I, the Lord, do all these things."[32]

After several more therapy sessions, the same counselor asked me if I were open to repeating the visualization exercise, the one that did not turn out so well a few paragraphs ago.

This time it was different. It did not take long in the next

---

[32] Isaiah 45.7

session to take up where the previous visualization had ended with a hostile standoff with Jesus. Jesus was still standing where I saw Him before.

"Toby," he said, and I immediately recognized The Voice as the One I heard decades earlier in the Seminary Chapel.

"I am the One that sends you into these horrific atrocities," he continued. "You did not recognize me. I clothed myself in darkness."[33] There was plenty of darkness around. "Your lap was my lap," he paused, as the faces of Arzil, Carlos and the others who have died in my lap scrolled through my mind.

"Your eyes were my eyes," he said softly. "I saw what you saw," as Jesus was acknowledging the things that I could not unsee. My heart began to soften.

"Your words of comfort to those who were hurting were my words." Now his words comforted me.

"Toby, you took your light to very dark places. Your light was a special light. Wherever you took your light, people found their way to me." There was a long pause between Jesus and me.

The counselor sat quietly, silently waiting for whatever would happen next. After several minutes, I spoke.

"Lord, thank you for telling me that you were with me even in those dark places." My need to know what God was doing

---

33 Psalm 18.11

revealed my lack of trust.

In my mind's eye, Jesus stood exactly where I had previously told him not to come any closer. Now he looked Middle Eastern. Along with his more realistic appearance I felt like my expectations of him were changing. Whereas before, I was asking "why?" questions, but now things were different. They did not seem to matter anymore.

"Please, sit next to me," I invited. He stepped over to the couch and sat next to me. With my eyes still closed, I turned my head to face him. "Thank you for being with me... for making me who I am, a Disaster Pastor... for giving me a special light and for sending me to very dark places."

Being honest with God, even when it feels irreverent, is an act of truth-telling that God honors. Giving ourselves permission to verbalize our anger to God about being angry at God allows us to examine if our anger might be a result of a conflict of expectations.

Do not worry about being impolite with God. Our anger does not faze God. To God, expressing our anger must be like watching us throw snowballs at the sun!

This long journey of listening to my Human Cry by being honest with myself and with God restored the intimacy I sought and created a brighter light.

45   Coming Home

Oh, happy day! I am leaving this latest hellhole and going home. The reason I always want to go home is simple; home is safe, clean and happy. Home is where I have my wife Judy, where I am near to my son Erik, his wife Allison, our two marvelous greatly-loved grandchildren and our friends.

At home, I know how things work. Nothing is broken that cannot easily be fixed. Life is predictable, clean and secure. I do not have to be vigilant or fearful. I know the rituals. I can relax. Home is life-giving. I always want to make it back home.

However, it does not take long to feel bored. There is nothing to get my adrenaline pumping: no threats, no hazards, no one shooting at us. It is as hard to re-enter the normal routines of everyday life as it is to enter a war zone. It takes time to gear down and not be hyper vigilant with everything that moves or pops.

People cannot relate to my stories. Their eyes glaze over and they want to change the subject.

After awhile I need to hear the Voice, or anyone's voice who will send me to the next disaster. I cannot explain why I feel compelled to go. Something calls out and pulls me to drop everything and "report for duty."

I know what awaits me out there, including the acts of evil men who take advantage of the absence of rules, law and order. I know that the deep, deep sorrows of the many new faces will remain etched in my mind.

Yet, if a disaster is going to happen, I feel the need to be there and do what a Disaster Pastor does—listen, pray and be a peaceful presence for all who have genuine needs.

There will be no escape from the sights, smells and the sounds of both the disaster and the Human Cry. Despite knowing that damage may seep into my soul and permanently attach itself to me, this is true: I love a disaster!

Whenever I enter into the next field of human misery, I welcome and embrace the victims' pain and suffering. In return, the darkness pulls back and my little light shines brighter.

I have become a better person and a higher-impact pastor because of lessons learned on disaster teams and serving as a Law Enforcement Chaplain.

Trial and Error are no longer cruel masters to be avoided; instead I welcome them as friends.

Now, I have learned how to work in the darkness and I trust that my little light will show the pathway for those "walking through the valley of the shadow of death." (Psalm 23)

Report 46 What Would You Do?

Several years ago I participated in a disaster scenario held at Laguna High School in Sacramento, California, a large spread out campus with numerous detached classroom buildings.

One special exercise included active shooters who held hostage a dozen students in a classroom building. A long 75 foot sidewalk stretched between the two buildings.

Throughout the day, many scenarios involved gunshots using simulation bullets, flash bang grenades and smoke filled air. I could not image a more realistic drill.

One exercise required an officer to run the distance of the sidewalk towards the target building. Immediately upon leaving the safety of the main campus, active shooters began firing at the approaching officer.

The only obstacle in his way was a student stretched across the sidewalk with very realistic moulage (pretend) stomach wounds. He had to jump over the student and dodge bullets until he reached a sheltered corner of the building. Leaping over the student at full stride he heard a voice. . . one he recognized.

"Dad, I'm hurt," said the voice beneath him. "Help me," he pleaded. Midstride he looked down and in horror recognized his son, bleeding and wounded.

Unbeknownst to the officer was that his biological son was a participant and intentionally picked to play a special role. The planners wanted to test how an officer might act when given an impossible choice. It was decided ahead of time that no penalty would be assigned to the officer for whatever action he took.

Instantly, the father/officer realized he was in a terrible dilemma. Should he tend to his son? Or, continue his task to set the other students free? He had to decide if his primary responsibility was to be a father or a SWAT officer.

What would you do?

Acknowledgments

- Rev. Dr. Tom Patterson, who is the most graced man I have ever known and the best Personal Coach. Thank you for helping me get unstuck.
- Ron and Darin Mittelstaedt, for providing me the time to write this book.
- Jay Hansell, whose professional skills as editor, writer, director, and producer made all the difference.
- Dave Lipin, the Commander of the DMAT CA-6 team, for leading us to hell and back time after time, for giving me the privilege of serving as the Padre and who gave life to several of these chapters.
- Rev. Dr. William Rapier is probably the bravest man I know. His father abandoned him on the day he was born… so Bill sets up orphanages in war-torn African countries. He is the Director of African Leadership Development.
- John Summers, who skillfully helped me become a better writer.
- Lora Stansbarger, who added detail, vibrancy, and pathos to many of the chapters.
- Ron Buckout, whose military handle was Bear, gave me the honored name, The Padre.
- Chief John Foster and Officers of the Grass Valley, CA, Police

Department, where I thoroughly enjoy serving as Police Chaplain, as well as Nevada City Police Department and the Nevada County, CA, Sheriff Department, where I do death notifications.

- Dr. Michael Finegan, who taught me fierce courage.

- Colonel Michael Foster, a Ranger with the 173st Army Airborne, who is the model of servant-leadership.

- Robert Sibert, former Director of the FBI Disaster Task Force, for his expert review. He currently leads the Chemical Forensics Program - Chemical and Biological Defense Division Science and Technology Directorate Department of Homeland Security.

- Susan Gabriel who edited it to death and gave it life.

- Colleen Dalton, who used her skill as a technical manuscript editor to catch what we missed.

- Precious members and staff of Kirkpatrick Memorial Presbyterian Church, First Presbyterian Church of Hayward, Folsom's Journey Church and Sierra Presbyterian Church, who supported me and always prayed for my safe return.

- My son Erik and his family, wife Allison and their children, who, along with my wife, Judy, are the great loves of my life.

Contact

I started out hoping this book would be a gift to you, especially in terms of listening to the Human Cry. I would welcome your comments and reviews. You can contact me at

Rev. Dr. Toby Nelson

First Response Chaplains of California

14806 Echo Ridge Drive

Nevada City, CA 95959

530-264-6644

tobynelson46@aol.com

www.disasterpastor.com

Made in the USA
Lexington, KY
01 July 2016